DANGER
IN THE
SEA

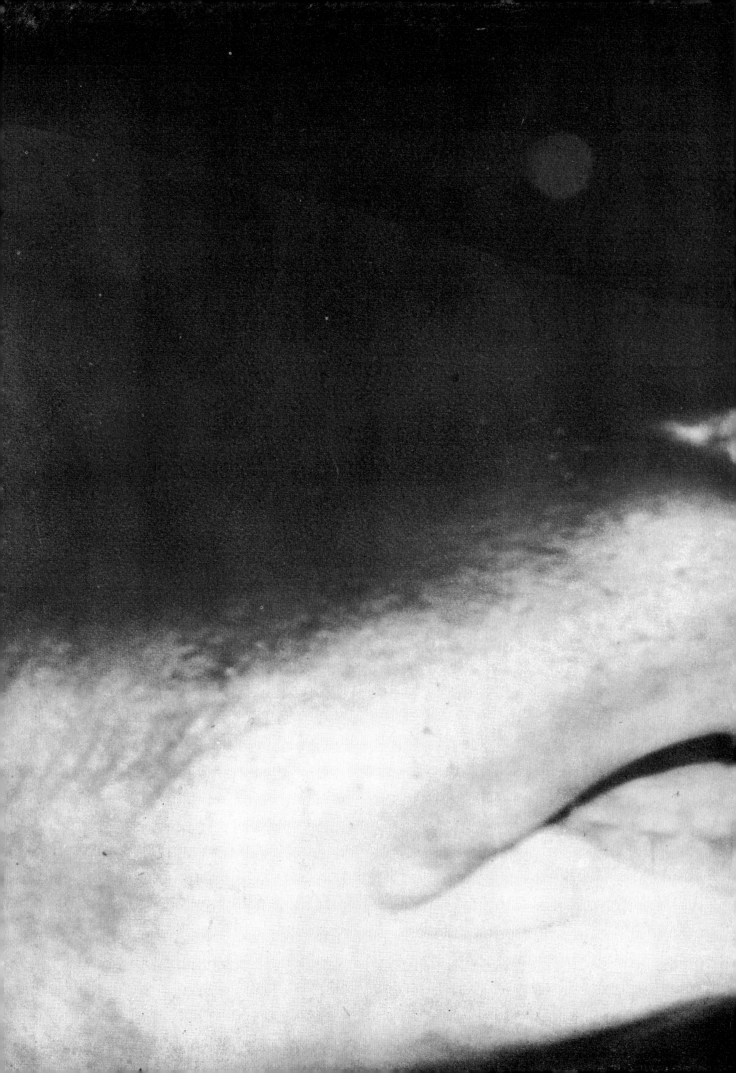

DANGER
IN THE
SEA

Alec Fraser-Brunner

Hamlyn
London New York Sydney Toronto

Published by The Hamlyn Publishing Group Limited
London · New York · Sydney · Toronto
Hamlyn House, Feltham, Middlesex, England
Copyright © The Hamlyn Publishing Group Limited, 1973

ISBN 0 600 32876 7

Phototypeset by Keyspools Limited, Golborne, Lancs.
Printed in Spain by Mateu Cromo Artes Grafias S.A., Madrid

Contents

Introduction 6

First things 8

Polyps and medusae 18

Shellfish 38

Octopuses and squids 44

Starfish, sea urchins and sea cucumbers 52

Sharks and other killers 60

Aggressive fish 91

Poisonous and venomous fish 100

Electric fish 116

Sea serpents 120

Further reading 126

Acknowledgements 126

Index 127

Introduction

It is only fair to state that this is not just a book about danger: it is a dangerous book. You must be warned that carefree holidays in the sea, splashing about in the sparkling waves or exploring the mysterious depths with a snorkel, will never be the same again—and indeed there is even a danger that if you are imaginative you will not venture into the sea any more.

This is a general account—not exhaustive by any means—of the varied assemblage of animals potentially harmful to man. A little is said about some things that originate in the sea and are dangerous to eat, but on the whole the story concerns animals we may meet when immersed in the water. Plants scarcely come into the picture. There are some microscopic floating kinds that may multiply under conditions favourable to them at such a rate that they kill all other aquatic life in that particular area (they contain a poison ten times stronger than strychnine); but that is all I need to say about them. The animals command the stage and seen altogether between these covers they are a frightening lot.

The only way to be absolutely sure of not encountering any of these dangers is to keep out of the sea, but I would certainly not follow that advice myself. The sea has so many wonders and beauties, even among its killers. As reassurance I can only state that in all my long, adventurous and no doubt ill-spent life I have been dabbling about in or on the sea, sometimes actually handling the things that are soon to be described, without even a scar to show for it.

Those who are born and bred to the sea and make their living by it are well aware of its potential dangers and treat it with great respect. The people who do foolhardy things or take unnecessary risks are usually landlubbers on holiday or engaged in sport and thousands of them die by drowning every year.

Apart from anything that lives in it, the sea itself is a stupendous force to be reckoned with. A human being entering this world of swirling movement and vast pressures is at a tremendous disadvantage. His muscles are no match for strong currents and may be cramped by temperature, his body is not armoured against collision with rocks and razor edged marine growths, he can neither breathe nor see properly underwater and his circulation is affected by pressure.

The sea is a sphere of the earth's environment where we do not belong; we have evolved over a great span of time as land animals. To find any other primate in the water is exceptional. If we insist on entering this alien habitat, even assisted as we are nowadays with artificial means of transcending our shortcomings, we have to be prepared to take the consequences.

The first of these is the possibility of drowning. The greatest toll of lives taken by the sea in all parts of the world is simply by drowning. But in addition to this the oceans are inhabited by a host of plants and animals that were already fully evolved there before man came into existence. They live in a world familiar to them, in which they act and react on one another while retaining a general pattern that, though changing in detail, remains essentially the same over aeons of time.

All these organisms are adapted to the life they live in the saline, shifting waters of the ocean. Man is not; and if he moves into their world he is a stranger, as unexpected an intruder as a monster from outer space would be to us. We need not be surprised, and should not blame them, if they react to us as we would to the monster.

It is a remarkable thing that such multitudes of people can swim happily in the sea, year in, year out, without being maimed or destroyed by its inhabitants. Leaving aside those invertebrates that can kill us without even comprehending our existence, most of the animals avoid us. Because we are not part of the ecology we are to them an unknown quantity, arousing either fear or, at the best, curiosity.

They may well consider *us* the danger in the sea—and with good reason. *Homo sapiens* is the most dangerous and destructive animal that has ever appeared on the surface of the earth. It is lucky for us that the inhabitants of the sea do not know what manner of beast it is that swims in its goggles and trunks and frog-feet with a harpoon gun in its hand, taking life not for necessity but for 'sport'; otherwise the roll of marine fatalities would be very much longer.

All things considered, we get off very lightly in our ever increasing invasion of this alien world. We incur the risk of dreadful agony and gruesome death, but the toll is extremely low in relation to the number of swimmers and compared with the proportion of tragedies on land. In a world of three thousand million people it is unlikely that injury or death by any one of the perils described in this book will amount to more than two hundred in a year. Compare that with the motoring statistics for one day in any modern city and it will be seen that, apart from drowning, the risks in the sea are very small.

First things

From our boat chugging along the Red Sea we can see several tall, twisting spirals of brown sand – miniature tornadoes – winding their way down the coast towards the south. Even well out to sea a fine film of sand settles on any flat surface of the boat. Aden, away over the sill, will lie in a golden fog and the sand will build up in thick layers as fast as it can be swept off the tabletops and chairs. It is intensely hot, for the khamsin is blowing, and even at sea there are mirages. The air dances over the glittering sea, and yellow sandbars appear to shuffle about so that it is difficult to tell just how near they are. Away on the coast the red pinnacles appear, disappear, wave as though doing a belly-dance.

The Red Sea gets its name largely from the bordering landscape which provides a backcloth of dramatic peaks and escarpments that glow golden red at most times but near sundown may attain the colour of blood. The sea itself is usually deep blue, but there are times when it too may become bright red in places, though during the khamsin this is more likely to be happening out in the Gulf of Aden, whither the hot, saline water of the Red Sea is being driven. This 'red tide' is very likely the kind of phenomenon that turned the waters of the Nile 'to blood' and made it poisonous in the Exodus story and it is due to a sudden blooming of unimaginable numbers of microscopic protozoa.

If we trace the evolution of animals back to the most simple that we know, we find that many of them have characteristics that make it diffi-cult to explain why they are animals and not plants. They are animate all right, moving about quite quickly at times, and they eat other small organisms after the fashion of the well-known *Amoeba*; but they also possess pigments similar to the chlorophyll that makes plants green and enables them to *make* their food from simple chemical substances with the aid of the energy obtained from the sun. This process, known as photosynthesis, is specially the property of most plants and so some botanists lay claim to these microscopic creatures. They belong to a mixed bag of things left over from very ancient days, when life had not proceeded beyond a single cell of protoplasm that was being modified in various experimental ways. Many of these, such as the diatoms, are indisputably plants, but others show features we associate with animals: we may best call them 'plant-animals'. They belong to the phylum Protozoa – 'first animals' – which includes *Amoeba*, the slipper-animalcule and *Euglena* of our ponds, and the foramins that formed our chalk cliffs; but here we are concerned only with a group called dinoflagellates.

It is obvious that there had to be plants on the earth before there could be animals, but at some stage in the story some of the early, single-celled plants began to take in smaller ones as an economical way of supplementing the results of their own photosynthesis. They thus started the process that ultimately gave rise to the great division into plant and animal kingdoms. But the primitive plants and the plant-animals did not die out. On the contrary, they are still represented by populations far exceeding any among the more elaborate groups – and quite able under certain conditions to wipe out the complicated mess they started so long ago.

Today, if we study the economy of the sea we find that the diatoms and other phytoplankton, which convert nitrates, silicates, phosphates and other salts by photosynthesis into organic matter, are the basic source of all the food in the ocean. Wherever the mineral salts are richest and within reach of sunlight, will flourish vast numbers of these tiny plants upon which other organisms may browse. However, in warmer waters, where the salts tend to be less accessible, their place is often taken by certain of the protozoa, which can acquire food ready-made when photosynthesis is difficult. Prominent among these are the dinoflagellates, so called because they propel and manoeuvre themselves in the water by means of two 'whips'. One of the whips moves across from side to side, operating somewhat like a paddle used alternately on each side of a canoe; the other trails behind and behaves as a stern oar or rudder. Often these lie in deep grooves so that the cell may have a sort of cross cut in it.

These organisms normally reproduce by division and so are sometimes found in chains of two, four, eight and so on. This happens when the water is warm; at low temperatures they tend to sink to the bottom and case themselves in a cyst until better conditions prevail. With the right temperature and an influx of food, they emerge from their cysts and join the plankton. If the conditions are specially favourable they may multiply so fast as to give rise to a local population explosion with disastrous effects.

This generally occurs in coastal waters where rich chemical nutrients encourage a dense growth of plankton or where such rich water rises up from the depths against a steep slope. It is very liable to happen in the Red Sea and Gulf of Aden, the waters of which are divided by a sill, a shallow area over which there is a reversal of water flow with a change of wind. Cool water comes from the Indian Ocean bringing a variety of living things including dinoflagellates which, finding themselves in the warmer and saltier Red Sea, proliferate rapidly. Then, with the wind from the north, water spills out into the Gulf, stimulating a rapid growth of protozoa there too. So in both areas there may be a sudden bloom of dinoflagellates in such numbers that the water actually changes colour – mostly red but sometimes other hues according to the chemistry of the organism.

Although no case where dinoflagellates have directly affected man has

been authenticated, they do contain a toxin which is lethal to other
animals such as fish. They are therefore of much concern to fisheries
and in some tropical areas it is believed that fish that have died under
such conditions are poisonous to eat. Certainly molluscs such as
mussels and clams become poisonous in a similar way. It was long ago
noted that outbreaks of 'paralytic shellfish poisoning' often followed
the appearance of discoloration in the sea and it has now been shown
that this is due to the molluscs feeding on the abundance of dinoflagellates presented to them in this way. Unfortunately, although there
are many recorded instances of human poisoning through eating

A patch reveals the presence of vast numbers of the protozoan *Noctiluca scintillans,* which often accompanies the poisonous *Gonyaulax* and may itself be toxic.

molluscs, it cannot always be established just what was eaten by the mollusc. Research on both coasts of America has pinned some blame on *Gonyaulax tamarensis* in the North Atlantic and *G. catanella* in the North Pacific. Species of *Gymnodinium* have been indicted off Florida and South Africa and *Pyrodinium phoneus* in the North Sea. Whether these or others were responsible for the many British cases we do not know. The symptoms are much the same so it may be that only a few kinds of dinoflagellates are able to pass the poison to us through shellfish.

The effect on humans is a general paralysis since the toxin acts upon both the central and the peripheral nervous systems. There is shortage of breath and gasping, with a fall in blood pressure. Death does not necessarily result but if it does it is due to the effect upon the brain and to paralysis of the cardiac muscles causing heart failure.

Bearing in mind that temperature controls dinoflagellate activity to some extent it is wise not to eat mussels or clams during the warm months of the year. Bright luminescence in the sea is a sign for caution, because *Gonyaulax* often accompanies the light-producing *Noctiluca*, which itself has been shown to contain a toxin.

While we are dealing with one-celled creatures it may be well to point out that bacteria – plants that can nourish themselves very well without the aid of sunlight – receive little mention in this book, despite their evil reputation as the 'germs' that carry disease. What needs stressing is that for every kind of bacterium that can do us harm there are many that do us a lot of good. We use them in many important processes of food production and waste disposal. Practically all the higher animals including ourselves carry an assortment of them about in the body and in many cases could not do without the work they perform. In the sea we can discount them as a problem, for there is small chance of a bacterial disease being passed directly from a marine creature to ourselves.

Scarcely anything could be more harmless than the bath sponge. Nevertheless there are other kinds of sponge that can inflict a certain amount of discomfort on swimmers exploring the areas in which they live. Sponges of one sort or another are to be found everywhere in the sea from the polar regions to the tropics, in shallow water or deep, and also in freshwater. They are highly successful creatures, having survived almost unchanged from the earliest ages of animate history, the Pre-Cambrian.

Basically, a sponge is a very simple thing – a kind of filter whose main feature is a special cell, the choanocyte, which contains numerous little whips that lash the water to keep it moving. The water is drawn in through a small opening, thereby preventing entry of large particles. It then passes through a fine strainer, the 'collar', that eliminates particles that are still too large to be digested, leaving only small organisms such as bacteria. There is no organized digestive system: the food is absorbed through the cell wall. Eventually the water, relieved of its nutrients and charged with the waste products, is driven out through a larger hole.

This simple structure is usually just multiplied as the sponge grows, so that it comes to have a large number of holes drawing in water and fewer, much larger holes expelling it. Sponges are so simply formed that it is difficult to recognize them as animals: they are permanently fixed to the substrate and show no movement. They are often brightly coloured and not uncommonly the colouring is due to algae or bacteria that live in the tissues, possibly to the benefit of both parties.

Most often a single sponge is both male and female. The male spermatozoan travels with the incoming current and is captured by a choanocyte which may take charge of it or pass it to a wandering cell (amoebocyte) that carries it around until it finds an ovocyte. The result of this union is a minute larva that propels itself in the water by means of cilia, very much like a ciliate protozoan. But it does not swim freely for long. As soon as a suitable site is found it settles nose down and develops into a plant-like animal.

The growth thus established can also reproduce by buds. Some amoebocytes travel to the surface of the sponge and form small pimples

Pages *13, 14 and 15* Spicules, greatly enlarged, taken from various sponges show the remarkable shapes they may attain. Though very small, they can be highly abrasive.

which grow out on stalks. These drop off, falling around the base of the parent, where they increase in size. In certain unfavourable conditions small, tough buds called gemmules grow around the base, so that if the parent should be damaged or destroyed they can, when circumstances improve, continue the existence of the colony.

Many different forms are assumed by sponges – they may stand up as a neat vase, grow to a huge cup, lie around as globes, branch upward like a tree, encrust a stone like a mess of cold porridge, or simulate a bloated hand. It is often difficult to recognize a species at first sight because it may take different forms according to the nature of the environment. Over four thousand species have been named. The best way to know them is to examine the spicules under a microscope.

Spicules are limey or siliceous structures secreted by sponge cells (probably to get rid of indigestible material in the first place) forming a web-like skeleton that helps to support the tissues. They are lovely things when magnified, displaying a variety of shapes which range from simple needles to bent pins, hairpins, horseshoes, stars, wheels and so on, and are constant enough to show an expert what species he is dealing with. These spicules generally make a sponge too prickly and brittle to be of use to mankind, though they provide a nice, heavily armoured hiding-place for a host of smaller creatures. Such sponges are, on the whole, immune from attack, partly due to their spicules and

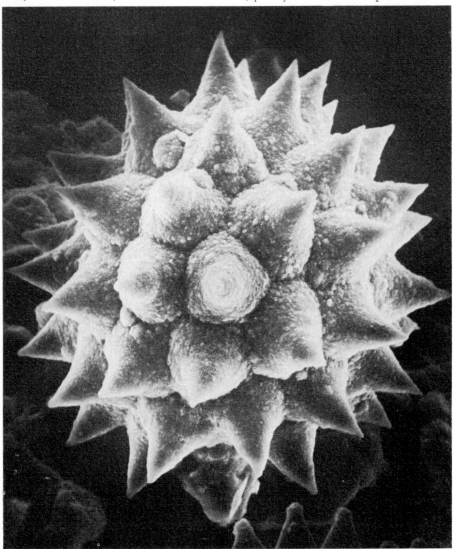

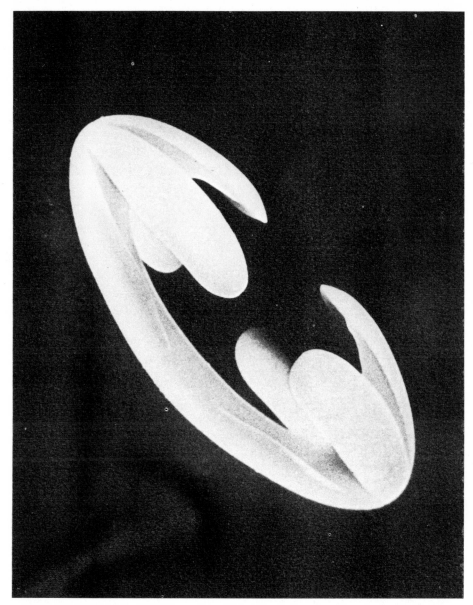

partly due to their exuding a poison with a repellent smell. Many
species have been found to possess toxic substances that are not dangerous to man. These may be put to good pharmaceutical use when
extracted: several valuable antibiotics have been obtained from them.

On the other hand, there are sponges that can be very troublesome
to swimmers invading their habitat. Generally their effects are due to
handling. The purple, billowing lobes of *Fibulia nolitangere* in the West
Indies can sting the hands badly and cause them to swell up. A closely
similar species is reported to do the same on Australian coasts. In
cooler waters, notably along the northeastern coast of the United
States, the bright scarlet fingers of *Microciona prolifera* cause localized
paralysis resulting in rigidity of the fingers, with swelling of the hand.
Acute dermatitis develops and must be treated at once or it may spread
and become very serious. Oyster fishermen often fall victim to this
sponge. The fire sponges (*Tedania*) are also bright red, as their name
suggests, and exude a substance that is poisonous to most marine animals. *Tedania ignis* occurs off Florida and *Tedania toxicalis* off California.

In general, the effects of sponge poisoning are a stinging sensation,
erythaema and dermatitis. Whether actual pricking by the minute

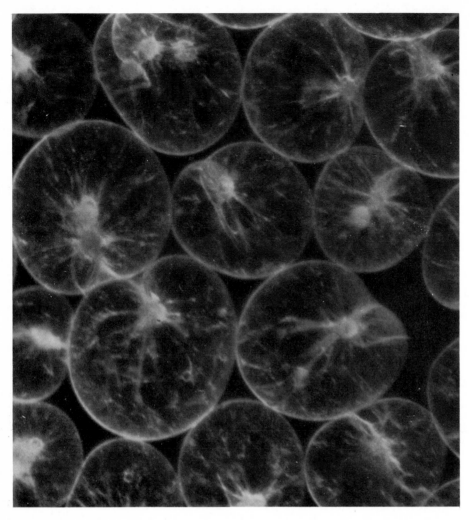

Left Responsible for much of the luminescence of the sea at night, the dinoflagellate *Noctiluca scintillans* often occurs in stupendous numbers. A few are shown here enlarged.

Right Typical sponges growing on a reef in Mauritius along with green sea anemones. The large exhalant apertures are a prominent feature.

Below right A stinging hydroid, *Lytocarpus,* growing above a fire sponge, *Tedania.*

spicules is involved or whether the action is entirely chemical has not yet been established. In any case it is wise not to handle sponges without gloves. In the event of toxication, weak vinegar is often a good immediate treatment; calamine lotion is also soothing. Antiseptic dressing should be applied as soon as possible, and in severe cases antibiotics and medical care may be necessary.

The bath sponge belongs to a small group in which the spicules have been more or less entirely replaced by spongin, a fibrous material that strengthens the tissues without making the structure brittle. The soft parts of the sponge, with the large amount of extraneous debris that has collected in the pores, have to be removed before it is saleable: it is only the fibrous skeleton we use.

Even this sponge is not without its hazards, however, for quite often a sea anemone, *Sagartia elegans*, is found attached to the basal parts of these sponges and can prove unpleasant to the people who collect them from the sea bed. A sponge diver usually puts his fingers beneath the sponge to separate it from the surface to which it is attached. The hand thus contacts the anemone, which replies with a broadside from its stinging cells. They are not powerful enough to kill the diver or even hurt him; he may not even notice them. But after several such encounters his hands become red and swollen with an unpleasant dermatitis and he may experience the headaches and vomiting often caused by anemone-type stings. In the Mediterranean this has long been known as 'sponge fishers' disease'.

Polyps and medusae

Despite the publicity given to dramatic monsters such as sharks and giant octopuses, the risk from these to the ordinary holiday maker is almost nonexistent, whereas much smaller – and often pretty – creatures that may be encountered on almost any beach at certain seasons provide a greater and in some ways more unpleasant hazard.

Who has not, when wandering along a beach at low tide, come across a stranded jellyfish – just a helpless blob of jelly drying out in the sun and wind – a rather pathetic creature? The temptation is to prod it, for it wobbles and quivers in a way that fascinates children, but it is advisable not to do this with the hands and not to let the children try to pick it up. Push it with the toe of a boot or with a stick if you must. It may be harmless but on the other hand it may be capable of stinging. If it is pinkish in colour and fairly large across the disc (anything from twelve inches to three feet) it is likely to be a *Cyanea* and if you were to meet it in the sea it would appear as a purplish, semi-transparent, inverted saucer pulsating gracefully along with bushes of tentacles around its rim – tentacles capable of stretching downward for 50 feet or more. If those tentacles came against your skin they would produce a fiery pain and raise great weals wherever they touched, for in their tissues they carry great numbers of tiny structures known as nematocysts.

It is not easy to describe a nematocyst: there are many different kinds to be found among jellyfish, doing different jobs. The only sort we have to worry about is the one that stings us, but all of them appear to work on the same principle. If one takes a rubber glove, pushes in the fingers so that they are inside-out, and then blows sharply into the glove, the fingers will pop out again. This is the sort of explanation often found in books. But a nematocyst is not much like a glove: it has only one very long, thread-like finger in a flask-like capsule with no opening through which air can be blown. Under an appropriate stimulus (touching some living body) a fluid containing a poisonous substance is forced through the wall of the capsule, rapidly building up pressure and filling the coiled up, inverted, hollow thread so that it is thrust out violently. It has a dart at its tip so that it can pierce the skin and inject

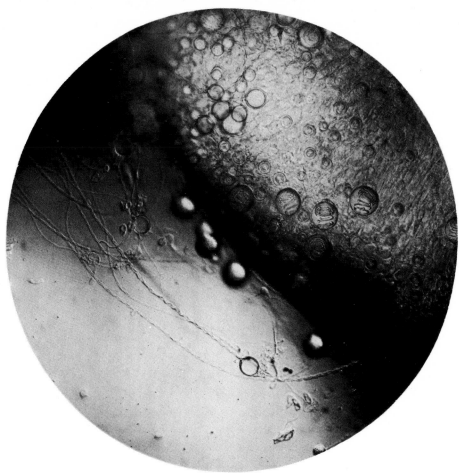

A portion of a tentacle of the Portuguese Man-of-war, showing undischarged nematocysts above with coiled threads clearly visible within them. Below the edge of the tentacle are discharged threads and empty capsules. Note the spiral of tiny barbs along each thread.

the venom. The thread usually has little spines arranged around it in a spiral, enabling it to attach itself or to wind itself around the prey and draw it up to the mouth. Although frightening, it is an intriguing mechanism. What is surprising is the complexity of the thing, considering that we are supposed to be dealing with very lowly and simple creatures.

A nematocyst is a tiny thing, scarcely visible without a microscope, but it does not operate alone. The lightest touch against a tentacle will trigger off a battery of hundreds or maybe thousands of these venomous darts, searing an area as though with a hot iron.

In recent years a good deal of research has been done in order to discover the details of the operation of nematocysts, but there is still a great amount to learn. The results of different workers appear contradictory at times and clarity is not helped by the fact that they are often working with different animals and different kinds of stinging cell. From the mass of information that is accumulating I have pieced together the following simplified account.

Firstly, although we call them stinging cells for convenience, the nematocysts are not themselves cells but are produced by the secretion of special cells known as cnidoblasts. But once formed, they behave like independent individuals that have taken up residence in the tissues of the animal. They are not under any nervous or muscular control: each one fires off its dart under a direct stimulus from outside. This stimulus is not tactile but chemical, for if a relatively inert substance like glass is brushed against a tentacle the nematocysts do not respond. A food substance – generally protein or fatty matter – is what turns them on. It seems there may be a sort of control through the cnidoblast (that

Above left Washed up on the shore, the beautiful Compass Jelly lies helpless.

Left The cypress-like *Aglaeophenia* is a tropical hydroid that can inflict severe stings on incautious swimmers.

Above A great bank of the coral *Millepora dichotoma,* whose polyps can be very dangerous to skin divers, photographed in the Red Sea.

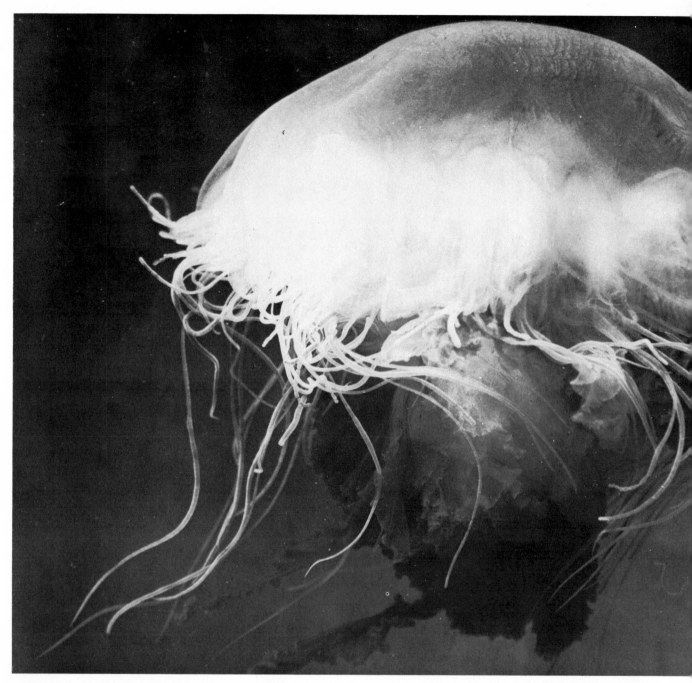

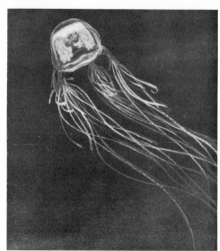

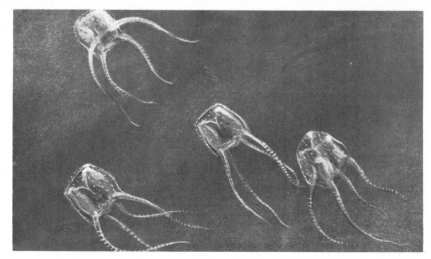

is the mother cell) because when the animal is fully fed the stinging apparatus does not work so well; it seems that if food substance is plentiful inside the tissues the flow of fluid is reduced and this prevents the nematocyst from functioning. But without this inhibition the presence of food on the outside causes a rapid intake of fluid that builds up considerable pressure. The thread, coiled inside-out in the capsule, is often pleated to reduce its volume and the barbs are crowded inside with their tips towards the centre. The capsular fluid now fills the thread, thrusting it rapidly outward; the pleats unfold so that the length of the thread is greatly increased as it everts and twists, spacing the barbs out in the characteristic spiral whorl round the outside; the long, hollow tube springs out straight, strengthened by the twist, and drives the dart at its tip into the source of food.

The discharge of the dart ruptures the capsule and the nematocyst cannot be used again. There are usually a number being formed in the cnidoblasts as a reserve, but exactly how replacement of used nematocysts by new ones is achieved has not yet been clearly shown. We may be sure that it is done rapidly and efficiently.

Extensive experiments with the contents of the nematocysts have shown that the capsular fluid is very complex, varying from one species to another. Unpleasant symptoms are produced by histamine and histamine-releasers, but in many cases the ingredient that does the most damage is found to be one or more of the polypeptides (proteins of low molecular weight); it is these that cause paralysis and death.

Because nematocysts often behave as though they are independent creatures lodged in the tissues of the jellyfish it is imprudent to handle even a specimen that appears to be dead (unless it is known to be a relatively harmless kind such as *Aurelia*) for the nematocysts may still be capable of stinging. Some kinds of nudibranch molluscs feed on these animals and can actually pass the nematocysts into special spaces in their skin, where they function on behalf of their predator. Sometimes after a storm when many jellyfish have been broken against the stones, fragments of tentacles may litter the beaches and it can be dangerous to walk with bare feet. This is particularly true in tropical regions.

Not all jellyfish are dangerous, of course. There are some 250 species known and most of them are either quite harmless to man or capable of producing only a mild prickling sensation. Quite a few of them are rare or inhabit parts of the world where humans are unlikely to contact them – like the enormous *Cyanea arctica* which can grow to 8 feet across, with tentacles reaching down for 200 feet, and which would be a frightful thing to meet if it did not inhabit water far too cold for humans to venture into. Certain kinds are even used as food in some parts of the world, for although they are mainly composed of water the jelly can have a surprisingly firm consistency. Some years ago a farmer had the bright idea of manuring his land with a great quantity of jellyfish that had been washed up on the coast nearby. He had them carted to the farm and spread out over the fields, never realising that 98 per cent of the carriage and labour had been expended on plain water; the things *looked* solid enough. However, we are here concerned with the kinds known to be dangerous and unless one has learned to distinguish it is advisable to regard them all with suspicion.

Jellyfish are, of course, not fish. They are properly called medusae and they belong to a rather lowly group of animals usually called

Above The Lion's Mane, *Cyanea capillata,* the killer of the Sherlock Holmes story. In this specimen the tentacles are retracted, showing the frilled mouth lobes clearly.

Far left The deadly cubomedusoid jellyfish *Chironex fleckeri* is probably the most dangerous animal in the sea.

Left Irukandji jellyfish, *Carukia barnesi,* are so small and transparent that swimmers are unaware of them until contact is made.

Right A Bluebottle, *Physalia utriculus,* floating in a rock pool. The bright blue bladder is a single, modified 'person', below which may be seen other persons (whether polyps or medusae is not certain) modified for swimming and feeding. A long, black tentacle is extended downwards.

Far right A closer view of the persons that make up the colony.

Below The float of the Portuguese Man-of-war, *Physalia physalis,* washed up on the shore is a beautiful object but best left alone.

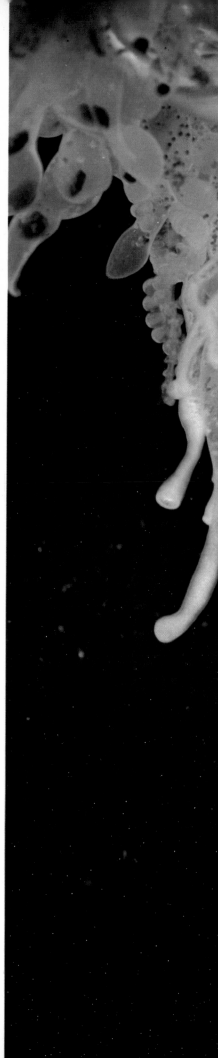

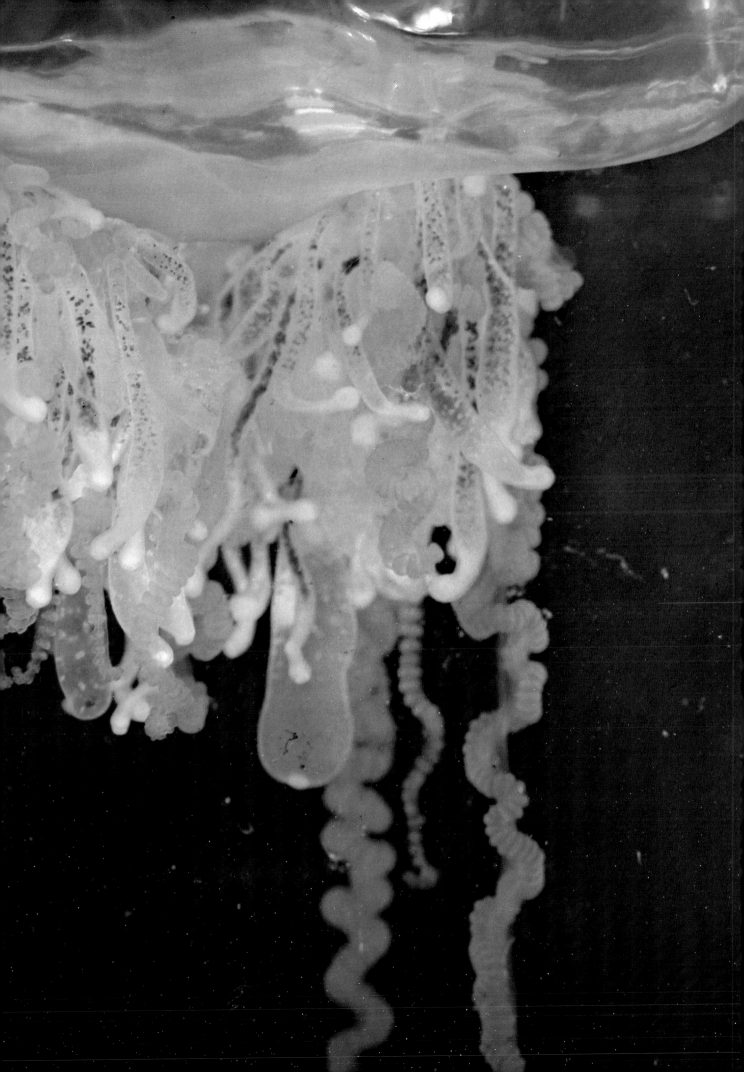

coelenterates, meaning literally 'hollow insides', but used to indicate that the body cavity is also the digestive organ. Roughly speaking, a coelenterate is just a stomach surmounted by a mouth surrounded by tentacles. The familiar sea anemones and the polyps that build the coral reefs are of this type while a jellyfish is essentially the same the other way up.

All these animals have cnidoblasts producing thread cells of one sort or another and no other group of animals possesses them. For this reason many modern zoologists prefer to call them Cnidaria. Very few of the eight or nine thousand species, however, possess nematocysts capable of penetrating the human skin and of those that do, the majority are medusae.

In the most primitive group of Cnidaria – called the Hydrozoa – we find small, anemone-like polyps. Without the aid of sex, hydrozoans produce large numbers of tiny medusae only a few millimetres in diameter, which swim away and join the plankton to become a menace to larval fishes. The medusae are bisexual, producing eggs and sperm; from their fertilized eggs come minute, swimming larvae called planulae which wander until they find a place to settle, when they develop into polyps and recommence the cycle. This basic arrangement, however, has many variations. Zoologists are currently arrayed in two opposing armies, electron microscopes at the ready, to decide which came first, the polyp or the medusa.

Few of the Hydrozoa cause inconvenience to man, but it is well to mention the hydrocorals or 'stinging corals' which may be encountered by swimmers in tropical waters. They differ from other Hydrozoa in forming great masses of limestone, so that they resemble the true corals. They are often in the form of pretty pink or violet branching stems that one is tempted to collect for the marine aquarium, but any attempts to do so will be rewarded with painful stings. Others are conspicuous features of the aquatic scene, building great spreading orange or brown blades like the antlers of a moose. Not for nothing is one of them called *Millepora alcicornis* – the Elkhorn Coral – often troublesome to skin divers off Florida and the West Indies, where another species, *M. platyphylla*, also occurs. Two others inhabiting the Red Sea and Indo-Pacific area are just as bad; occasionally one brushes against them when swimming through a reef, receiving a very unpleasant rash as a result. Sometimes they form encrustations on true corals and I once came to rest on one of these, receiving such stings as to make the wearing of trousers uncomfortable for a couple of days. The name 'fire coral' sometimes given them is not inappropriate.

Some hydrozoans are very plant-like, forming groves of pretty, waving fronds; but they are not plants, just colonies which build a flexible skeleton instead of a rigid, stony one. *Aglaeophenia cupressoides*, as its name suggests, rather resembles a cypress, though it is golden brown in colour. Groves of it are to be found not far from shore in many tropical areas. To push through such a growth is to invite a mass of red weals and blebs that may last for days. Others, such as *Pennaria*, do the same but it is not necessary to list them all in a work such as this.

These things are merely an irritation, to be avoided after a little experience. Some of the hydrozoan medusae can be more dangerous (though most of them are not). A notorious example is the orange-striped jelly *Gonionemus vertens*, occurring in the North Pacific, North Atlantic and Mediterranean. In some places it is common enough to be

A fire coral, *Millepora*, in the Red Sea. The expanded polyps give the branches a furry appearance.

Following pages Like some other
creatures in this book, the sea
anemone *Sagartia elegans* var *rosea*
is more beautiful to behold than
to handle. It is the cause of

sponge fisherman's disease in the
Mediterranean and elsewhere.
The typical form of an anemone,
with the mouth surrounded by
tentacles, is well shown here.

preserved in large numbers for use in teaching students the details of medusan anatomy. It lives among eel grass, adhering by means of sticky pads at the ends of its tentacles, but in the right conditions – calm weather and an overcast sky – it rises to the surface where it turns upside down, so that the mouth is uppermost like a polyp's and sinks slowly down again, spreading its tentacles wide to catch food. It is on such visits to the surface that it may encounter a cavorting human, who will promptly retire hurt. So far stings from *Gonionemus* have been reported mainly from the western Pacific – off Japan and the east coast of the USSR.

More widely recognized as a menace is the so-called Portuguese Man-of-war, *Physalia physalis*, of the tropical Atlantic and the Mediterranean. This is not a single animal but a colony of the hydroids called siphonophores. Both polyps and medusae are modified in various ways to do specialized jobs and all are coordinated to behave together like a single organism. The whole is kept at the surface of the sea by a gas-filled float, usually bright blue in colour, sometimes with streaks of orange-yellow – a beautiful object to observe from the safety of a boat. Below this there are polyps concerned with feeding and others with reproduction and swimming, while fifteen or more coiled tentacles bearing vast numbers of stinging-cells can be extended downwards to a depth of 100 feet or more.

The name Portuguese Man-of-war commonly applied to this elaborately organized engine of death, seems to stem from the fact that the Portuguese call it *Caravela*. It does not look much like a caravel to me, nor indeed like any sort of ship except a very tubby one floating keel upwards. Another species, *P. utriculus*, common in the Indo-Pacific region northward to Japan and Hawaii, has a float more like a flask and is accordingly called the 'Bluebottle' when washed up on Australian beaches. What it is called by those unfortunate enough to make contact with it is unprintable even in these permissive days.

Despite the float, *Physalia* is not always seen by the swimmer, for by adjusting the amount of gas it can sink below the surface. Even if seen it may already be too close. To brush against the tentacles is to be stung over a considerable area of skin by millions of venomous threads. According to F. E. Russell, 55,000,000 nematocysts weigh only 1 gram and over 62 grams of them are to be found in 1 gallon of tentacle tissue; how many gallons there may be of the jelly-like mass removed from the water depends on the size of the *Physalia*.

The damage this creature can do depends not only on its size, but on how well fed it is (as explained in the account of the stinging cells) and how much tentacle comes in contact with the skin. Even a mild contact is distressing but extensive stings from a large specimen are ruinous and may bring death within minutes.

Wherever a tentacle touches the skin it immediately produces intense pain by the injection of venom from millions of nematocysts. A great weal with a spreading red rash around it indicates the line of contact. Often the victim thrashes about in agony, thereby increasing the chance of tangling with other tentacles and thus extending the affliction. These effects, probably produced by histamines, are quickly followed by the paralytic action of the toxic proteins. In mild cases these may cause weakness, vomiting, muscular pains, increased perspiration and vertigo; in more severe cases there is respiratory difficulty, cyanosis and violent twitching, and the heart is stopped by paralysis of the system that stimulates it. The chance of survival after an extensive contact seems to be very small.

Portuguese Men-of-war, along with some other venomous medusae, are common in the Straits of Malacca, perhaps due to the set of the currents and the great abundance of marine life upon which they can feed. *Physalia* often appear in large shoals in the middle of the strait. Strangely enough, during eight years spent in that region, I heard of only one fatal encounter. A young boy swimming not far from the shore suddenly screamed and splashed about and his parents, not knowing what was the trouble but suspecting a shark, fetched him in hurriedly. He died as he was brought up the beach and the appalling weals on his body left no doubt as to the cause of the tragedy.

Some experiments suggest that a mild dose of *Physalia* toxin injected beforehand acts as a prophylactic against a stronger dose, in the manner of an inoculation. An injection of isotonic potassium chloride is said to serve a similar purpose. But as a meeting with *Physalia* is generally unpredictable such recommendations are not very helpful.

Immunity to the stings does seem to be developed by some animals. The young of the Blanket Octopus actually use pieces of Portuguese Man-of-war tentacle as defence and to kill their prey. There is a small fish, *Nomeus*, that commonly lives with *Physalia* and, indeed, is never found anywhere else; it has only to retreat among the trailing tentacles to be quite safe from enemies and it may be that a pursuing fish is thus lured for the benefit of the host. It is said to browse upon the tentacles that are so lethal to other animals, so presumably it demonstrates the prophylactic principle mentioned above.

Nomeus is not alone in seeking the protection of deadly stinging cells, however. Some of the fishes we use as food find shelter among the tentacles of medusae such as *Cyanea* mentioned at the beginning of this chapter. This is one of the disc jellies, the group most familiar to seaside visitors and most often observed from the decks of ships. The 'umbrella' is often beautifully coloured and is usually transparent enough to show the four-sided arrangement of the internal organs – four reproductive organs and four stomach sacs. Below the umbrella hang the mouth lobes, which often take the form of long frills that catch up the food seized by the tentacles. The margin of the umbrella carries sense organs and tentacles set in notches, which vary in number according to the species. The umbrella contracts and relaxes rhythmically, forcing the water from its concave side as it closes. The medusa is thus propelled convex side foremost, trailing the tentacles in its wake.

Jellyfish such as these are not just a stage in the life history of a polyp: they represent the main animal. The polyp stage may not occur at all; if it does, it is very small and the trunk soon divides into a pile of little medusae that separate off and swim away (or in some cases the polyp transforms directly into a medusa). So whereas in the hydroid Cnidaria the polyp is the thing and the jellyfish is just a means of spreading the population over the sea bed, in these true jellyfish or Scyphozoa the medusa is the thing and the polyp is only a brief stage in its development or may be eliminated altogether.

Most of the disc jellies are harmless or only slightly irritating, but there are some like the *Cyanea* already mentioned that must be rated as dangerous. In particular the Sea Nettle, *Dactylometra quinquecirrha*, is a notorious species that is found in all warm seas between about 40° north and 40° south of the equator, sometimes following the Gulf

Despite the nematocysts that can kill small fish, some fish – especially those of the genus *Amphiprion* – form partnerships with sea anemones. Usually a pair of fish will inhabit an anemone which will recognize that pair and reject others. The fish thus obtain the protection of the lethal armoury of the anemone and in return brings portions of food.

Stream to a more northerly limit. This medusa grows to about 8 inches across. Although pretty in appearance, with an opaline umbrella, pinkish mouth parts and golden tentacles, it is lavishly supplied with stinging cells that can cause extreme pain or death to a swimmer. The active agent in this case seems to be tetramine which has a powerful paralysing effect on the motor nerve endings. Even more beautiful in appearance is *D. pacificus*, which is purplish with radiating black markings and black tentacles; but it is equally if not more virulent, and has been the cause of many casualties in Japanese waters.

Most disc jellies, however, are fairly conspicuous, slow-moving creatures pulsating gracefully along at the surface. If a number of them is to be seen in the vicinity it is sensible not to go into the sea. They are less to be feared than the cube jellies (Cubomedusae), sometimes called sea wasps, which are in some ways the most terrible things we may meet in the sea. As the name implies, the four-way structure expresses itself on the outside, the sides being flattened so that the umbrella, viewed from above or below, looks square. In some of them the top is also rather flattened, resulting in a roughly cubical shape.

What makes these so alarming is that they are usually very small and transparent, and pulsate much faster than other medusae, moving through the water at great speed so that a swimmer does not see the missile that strikes him. One kind has given a lot of trouble on beaches along the coasts of Australia north of the Tropic of Capricorn, where there often occurs a sudden outbreak of distress in a small area, up to forty people being stung over a short period while nearby beaches remain unaffected. Such attacks usually last only a couple of days, but they might recur several times in a season.

This phenomenon was known to the aborigines and at first their name for it – irukandji – was adopted, for the cause of it could not be found. First the swimmer feels a sharp prickling on that part of him that is close to the surface of the water. This is followed after a few minutes by a pimply rash over an area larger than that first affected, which dies down again and is gone in less than half an hour. Meantime, however, other symptoms become apparent – acute backache, pains in the chest, abdomen and upper thighs, general weakness and tingling sensations and often aches in the armpits and groins as though the lymph system were affected. In more severe cases there is a tightening of the chest making breathing difficult.

A variety of lesser discomforts develop, such as headache, excessive sweating, vomiting, shivering and smarting eyes. A fairly effective treatment has been found for it – an intravenous injection of pethidine followed by a moderate dose of aspirin.

It was not until 1966 that Dr J. H. Barnes with a number of volunteers was able to devise special traps to catch the creature responsible for so much misery. He found tiny medusae – the largest was only $\frac{1}{2}$ inch in diameter and $1\frac{1}{2}$ inches long including the tentacles – which were absolutely transparent except for the reddish clusters of nematocysts which give a peppered appearance to the umbrella. Most of the nematocysts, however, are borne on rings or collars round the tentacles, the parts between the rings being flexible to allow for lengthening or shortening.

To make quite sure that this was the creature they sought, Barnes and his assistants heroically made contact themselves and experienced the irukandji syndrome. It is only fitting that, when this little terror was found to be previously unknown to science, it was called *Carukia barnesi*. The name irukandji for the syndrome has now been dropped in favour of carukiosis.

The epidemics are caused by a combination of geographical features, such as the Great Barrier Reef and sandbanks, and certain weather conditions that bring a great stream of medusae, ctenophores and salps near to the shore. When the water is found to be cooler and clearer than usual and the specific gravity 1.024 or higher, then many small jellyfish and ctenophores (jellies with threads that do not sting but are sticky) are likely to be present and salps may be stranded at the upper tide mark. In these conditions *Carukia* may also be there, so small and transparent and moving so quickly through the water that no swimmer is likely to see it.

A somewhat larger kind, *Chiropsalmus quadrigatus*, is known from the Indian Ocean, the north coast of Queensland and the Philippines. Although it is less likely to be a killer than was formerly thought, it is quite bad enough. It has six or more tentacles at each corner and these inflict very painful weals that often show a pattern formed by the rings of nematocysts. Rubbing or scratching must be avoided since cellulitis may result. Itching and discoloration of the skin may last for as long as six months.

The real villain of the piece is larger again – up to $4\frac{1}{2}$ inches from top to rim, with tentacles that can extend down for many feet, carrying one hundred to two hundred times the amount of venom possible for the previous animal. It produces similar weals, about $\frac{1}{4}$ inch wide, but the pain is more severe and lasts longer. There is much swelling and blistering and permanent scars may be left on the skin. Even in the milder cases discoloration remains for a very long time and periodic itching may continue for years. The victim is also left with a susceptibility to streptococcal infections. But the more severe stings often prove fatal. This cubomedusan sea wasp, *Chironex fleckeri*, is the most dangerous creature known to man, for its poison acts so fast that there is no chance to aid the victim of an extensive contact.

Fatal cases usually happen in shallow water when the bather is moving quickly – running, swimming, leap-frogging and so on – so that he becomes entangled with the tentacles before he has time to realise the danger. Then of course he tries frantically to free himself, making the sting wider and spreading it to his arms and hands, the meanwhile screaming with the pain which is instantaneous and extremely severe. He becomes frantic and makes for the beach, smothered in what appear to be thick cobwebs. Well-meaning people who try to help him only make matters worse and probably get stung themselves. In anything from one to three minutes from the first contact he collapses, twitches and shudders, and is dead. In two or three cases where it was possible to douche the wounds with alcohol or methylated spirits at the time of collapse the patient survived, albeit to suffer long disability. But usually the collapse is the end; any treatment must be applied before it happens.

Experiments on mice have shown that the venom of *Chironex fleckeri* is about three hundred and fifty times more deadly than that of the Portuguese Man-of-war, so it is undoubtedly the most dangerous creature to be found in the ocean. *Chiropsalmus* has been blamed for some of its misdeeds through confusion, having a similar range. Immature *Chironex* look very much like adult *Chiropsalmus*.

The best way to avoid either, if swimming within their range, is to

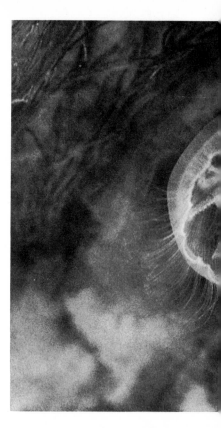

One of the commonest jellyfishes, often seen at the surface in large numbers, is *Aurelia*, whose stinging cells do not easily penetrate human skin and therefore produce only mild irritation to sensitive persons.

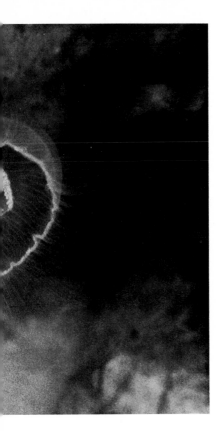

go into the water when waves are breaking on the shore and the surface of the sea is slightly choppy, for none of the cubomedusae favour these conditions; they prefer dead calm, oily-smooth water for their rapid invasions. Cool weather, with smooth seas and a landward flow caused by an island or sand-bar is the setting for a drift of medusae, cteno-phores and salps. On such a day keep a wary eye open.

There are other cube jellies that deserve mention, such as *Charybdea rastoni*, which is one of the throng that spoil the amenities of the Malacca Strait and eastward. It has relatives in the Atlantic and in the Pacific as has *Tamoya* of the same family. *Tamoya haplonema* sometimes gets as far north as New York.

The effects of jellyfish toxins seem sometimes to depend on the humans concerned. For example, I have handled *Aurelia* and felt nothing at all, whereas others complain of a nettle-like pricking. Again, the Mauve Jelly, *Pelagia noctiluca*, is said to produce painful weals, yet I once manipulated a number of them without ill result. *Pelagia* is luminescent and one night during a research cruise off the west coast of Ireland they were present in large numbers. The wash of the ship cast to either side a continuous stream of globes of greenish light. We put out tow-nets and they came back packed tight with the animals, some of which I preserved for the British Museum and others I put in a galvanized bath on the deck. For some time I experimented with these spheres of jelly – each about the size of a large orange and similarly dimpled all over. At the slightest touch they glowed with a bright, greenish-blue light that faded away until another touch was given. It was contact with the stem of the ship that caused them to blaze away in our wake. Some other people, perhaps less well endowed with anti-histamines, might have come out of it less happily. On the other hand the condition of the jellyfish might also have had something to do with it, for some kinds are known to be dangerous only during the breeding period. Either way, I count myself fortunate.

Anyone stung by jellyfish while in the water should get out of it as soon as possible, for the initial sensation is no guide to the actual toxication. Weakness and unconsciousness may follow, causing death by drowning.

It must be repeated that when medusae are known to be in the area it is unwise to go into the water at all; this is especially true in the tropics but danger can appear just as well in cooler water at times. If, when in the sea, a jellyfish is sighted, keep well clear of it, remembering that the umbrella is trailing tentacles for a long way behind it.

If contact is made, the first thing to do is to immobilize the nemato-cysts. This can be done by drying them with a powder – flour, talcum, dust or fine dry sand – then scraping off the tentacles. As much as twenty feet of tentacles have been removed from a patient who sur-vived. Do not rub or pluck the tentacles as this merely causes more nematocysts to discharge and increases the damage. The best thing is liberal swabbing of the whole area with methylated spirits, alcohol or diluted formalin (10 per cent), in order to fix the tissues of the tentacles and so put the nematocysts out of action. Until this has been done do not under any circumstances wash the area with fresh water. An injec-tion of pethidine given intravenously will relieve the pain. When stings are on the limbs apply tourniquets above them to delay absorption of the venom into the system. Do not rub the skin, and prevent the patient from moving about if possible. In the event of collapse, apply

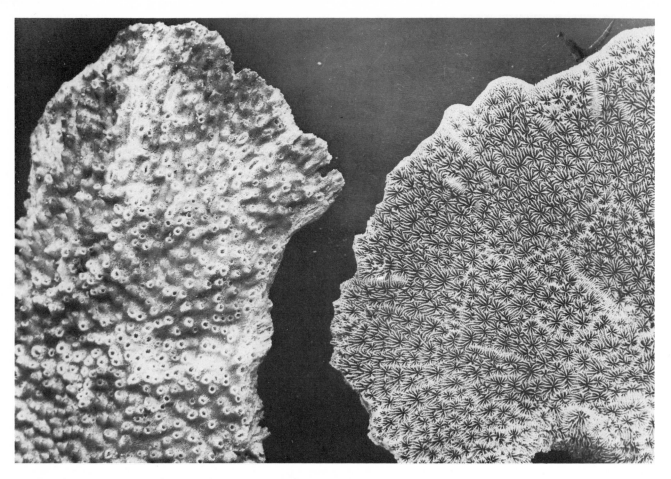

artificial respiration and the 'kiss of life' pending the arrival of medical aid. All cases should be taken to the nearest hospital immediately.

Of the true corals (Madrepores) and the sea anemones, a number are said to be capable of inflicting mild stings on sensitive people. Here again I have been lucky despite having to handle a number of species during work in public aquaria. In the tropics I have taken a number of the larger sea anemones to use as companions for the little clownfishes that live so happily with them, evidently being immune to the stings. I have prised them gently off the rocks with bare hands and brought them to the surface without the slightest discomfort.

There is, however, a harmful anemone, a species of *Sagartia*, which adheres to the basal parts of sponges. This affects the hands of the fishers when they place their fingers beneath the sponge to release it from its attachment, causing the 'sponge fishermen's disease' familiar in the Mediterranean and elsewhere. Moreover, a number of cases are on record of local inflammation set up on the skin by sea anemones, often developing into ulceration and taking a long time to heal. Sometimes nausea, headaches and other unpleasant general symptoms are also experienced.

Coral is troublesome not so much for the stinging as for the cuts and abrasions caused by the hard, rough edges. Any wound of this kind should be treated as soon as possible with iodine, TCP or something similar, for if left unattended it is liable to become septic. Calamine lotion is soothing. In bad cases dressings and antibiotic treatment may be required and qualified medical attention should be sought.

Taking it all round, the cnidarians, beautiful as they are, give a broad hint that we are not wanted in the sea.

Above Pieces of stony coral to show the holes in which the polyps dwell. Those on the right are elaborately sculptured to fit the shape of the polyps.

Right A bank of coral provides innumerable hiding places for fish, crabs and other creatures.

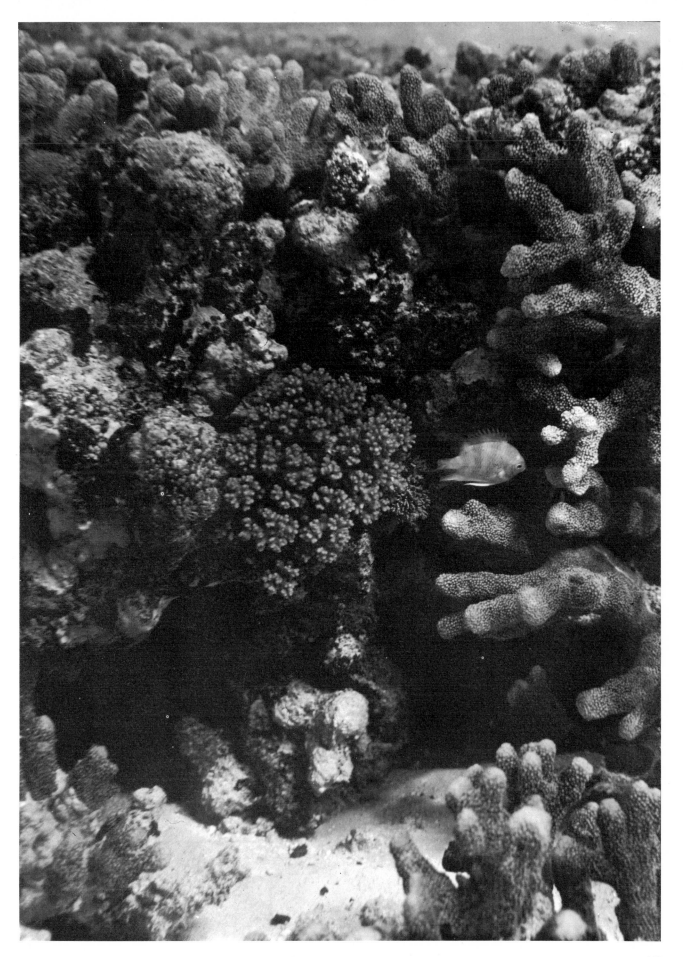

Shellfish

We are able to trace back the evolution of molluscs by way of a series
of worm-like creatures from the single-celled animals discussed earlier.
Worms themselves, although they abound in the sea in a great variety
of forms, do not really merit a place in this book: there are a few spiny
ones that can produce slight urticaria but none that really sting or bite.
Mention may perhaps be made of certain kinds of blood-flukes that
parasitize birds on Atlantic coasts and whose larvae are able to penetrate the human skin. The eggs leave the birds in their droppings and
develop inside various marine snails. When they reach the cercaria
stage they escape into the water. They should then dig their way back
into birds to become adult and begin the process over again; but often
they find burrowing into man just as satisfying, though they cannot
develop in him. Clam diggers, sea bathers and fishermen who are
attacked by these get a skin rash that can be so severe as to prostrate
them. The treatment is to dry the skin at once and stay out of the
water; the creatures will soon die off, for our blood conditions are very
different from those of birds.

Some mention of the molluscs as transvectors of poison produced by
dinoflagellates has already been made, so we need not touch again on
the results of eating them at the wrong time. Many of them, however,
are found to have poisons of their own and in most cases we have no
idea how they are used by them. Some 'sea hares' and some of the
murex family contain toxins that have been found to kill mice, but this
is not likely to be their real purpose. The saliva of some others such as
Neptunea consists of as much as 1 per cent of tetramine, which works in
conjunction with choline and its ester, and histamine. We have met
these powerful toxic agents among the jellyfish so we may guess what
happens to the prey of *Neptunea*. In fact it is not unlikely that this
mollusc gets the toxins ultimately from cnidarians. Some of its relatives, the aeolids or sea slugs, crawl over hydroids and corals feeding
on polyps which they digest all but the cnidoblasts. These deadly
weapons they are able to pass intact into their prominent appendages
and the mantle plumes which serve them as gills. The nematocysts, as

A Giant Clam, *Tridacna maxima,* becomes in time completely imbedded in the corals growing around it with just the mantle extruded through the gaping halves of the shell. When very large, the clam could snap tight on an intruding foot.

Mussels growing upon rocks and piles sift small organisms from the water which they inhale. Among these organisms may be the toxic protozoa mentioned in the first chapter which are ultimately responsible for shellfish poisoning. The sharp edges of the shells of mussels and some oysters are sometimes a hazard to swimmers.

Right This view of an Otter Shell shows the large siphon through which it draws in a stream of particles.

Below Some aeolid sea slugs are able to eat polyps and digest them without destroying or discharging the stinging cells. They can pass them to their own skins and use them for protection.

mentioned earlier, behave like independent bodies and will fire their
darts as readily for the aeolid as for the polyp. The amazing thing is
that the sea slug can demolish the polyp and transfer the stinging cells
without triggering them off. Just how effective this acquisition of the
venom of the cnidarians can be is proved by the fact that although
these creatures, which are related to snails, have no protective shell,
they are practically invulnerable and avoided as food by other animals.

Among the shellfish, however, the specialists in poison warfare are
some of the cone shells. To shell collectors cone shells are among the
most desirable possessions, with subtle lines, smooth surfaces and
beautiful patterns when cleaned. Very high prices are paid for the shells
of some of the less common species like the Glory-of-the-sea Cone,
Conus gloriamaris. The exact number of species in the genus *Conus* is not
agreed, but it is around four hundred.

When the animal is alive a goodly part of its shell is covered by the
mantle, which tends to make it less conspicuous. It lies in shadow under
coral heads or among the algae attached to coral reefs. Many, if not all
of them, come out to hunt at night. The food they seek varies, of
course, with the species; it includes polychaete worms, other molluscs –
gastropods, bivalves and little octopuses – as well as small fishes. The
cone detects its prey by means of chemoreceptors – that is by taste or
smell – and thereupon pushes out its proboscis carefully until contact is
made with the food. It instantly harpoons the prey with a venom-
charged harpoon that paralyses it. The proboscis then contracts and
draws back the helpless victim to the mouth, which can open quite
widely to engulf it.

When I said that the cone *harpooned* its prey I used the word deliberately. Anyone familiar with the old whaling methods of the *Moby Dick*
period is amazed when shown the venom apparatus of the cone, suit-
ably magnified. There it all is – the harpoon with shaft and barb, and
the line as well. One species even has a hinged tang, a refinement that
came comparatively late in whaling circles.

The harpoon is actually one of the teeth of the radula, the rasp which
is modified to various purposes among gastropods. In the cones and
their relatives the turrids and auger shells (Terebridae) – they are all
grouped together in the sub-order Toxoglossa – the radula is so
arranged that the teeth can be ejected as harpoons one at a time.

A close look at the harpoon is interesting. To see how it works the
easiest thing is to take a piece of foolscap paper and fold it lengthwise
in two, then, starting from the fold, roll it at an angle so that it forms a
round shaft; but when little more than half way cut away the remainder
except for a backward-pointing barb at the upper end. If the paper is
semi-transparent you have a large-scale approximation of the real thing.
The venom flows between the two parts of the folded paper and so
comes out near the point. In the original, the radular tooth is formed of
a horny material reminiscent of the shaft of a bird's feather. If imbedded
in something too large to be pulled back and swallowed the tooth is
abandoned and remains in the wound. There are plenty more teeth
ready to be brought into action.

None of the turrids or augers are dangerous to man and quite a few
of the cones are quiet, retiring into their shells when disturbed. The
largest of the cones, *C. millepunctatus*, has the smallest venomous equipment (the dart is only about one millimetre long) and so can do little
damage. On the other hand some kinds are aggressive, one of the worst

In close view the mantle of the Giant Clam shows small 'windows' through which sunlight enters. Here are cultivated the algae on which the clam depends for its food.

being *C. textile*, a common species that rummages among coral debris. This and some others have accounted for a number of human lives. The chemical nature of the venom has not yet been determined, but it has obvious effects upon the heart and respiratory system.

In view of the popularity of shell collecting and the demand for specimens of *Conus* it seems useful to give a list in alphabetical order of the species that have been known to sting human beings: *aulicus, californicus, geographus, gloriamaris, magus, marmoreus, omeria, stercus-muscarius, striatus, textile, tulipa.* All these could be fatal and there may be others of the four hundred or so that are potentially dangerous.

Giant clams appear from time to time in adventure stories, the two halves of the shell of these bivalve molluscs being represented as great jaws just waiting to snap upon an unwary diver and devour him. The Giant Clam, *Tridacna*, lying half-hidden by growth of other organisms, might conceivably be a trap for an unobservant person. It lies hinge down, often in a pocket in the rock or coral, with the valves of the shell half open, the brightly coloured mantle being extended between them as a wavy band. It seems, from recent researches, that it has no interest in catching anything, but a foot thrust into the mantle would be taken as a sign of danger and the shell would at once snap shut. Generally the clam is in very shallow water, so the person concerned would have to wait for help or until the clam thought fit to relax. In deeper water, however, the trapped person would be very likely to drown.

Today the risk of this is very remote indeed. *Tridacna* is becoming very scarce on reefs because of the demand for it by shell collectors and curio hunters. Large ones adorn rockeries in gardens, moderate-sized ones become bird-baths, lesser ones are ash-trays, and so on. Only those in relatively inaccessible places or those too heavy to be lifted without mechanical aid are allowed to remain in the sea. Specimens have even been imported alive for the tropical marine aquarium by ill-informed dealers.

Tridacna cannot live under the artificial light of the ordinary amateur aquarium. It must have strong sunlight for its well-being. The reason is that it depends for its nourishment upon algae which grow in spaces within the tissues. These spaces are illuminated by little windows, looking like tiny eyes, in the mantle. Strong sunshine is therefore essential in order to enable the algae to photosynthesize food materials which are collected by the white corpuscles in the blood-stream of the clam. So far as present knowledge goes, the clam is entirely dependent on this source of food and does not use its ordinary digestive system. It grows and harvests the algae like a crop in its sunlit chambers and the exposed mantle may vary in colour according to the state of the crop and the species being grown. It may be purple, bright green, and even orange or red.

In the great days of the seaside resort, with bathing machines and long piers, a favourite theme of the comic postcards that flourished at that time was a fat man, or an even fatter lady, leaping in the air with a large crab hanging on to his or her big toe. It was usually accompanied by a devastatingly witty caption such as 'There's a nip in the air here'. That is about all I have to say about crabs and their relations, the lobsters, in this book. Some of them, not least the Edible Crab, *Cancer pagurus*, have powerful claws and can pinch a pedal digit with considerable force. Otherwise, this marine armoured brigade is not to be listed among the great dangers of the ocean. It merely remains to repeat the advice given elsewhere – don't paddle or wade with bare feet.

The powerful claws of the Edible Crab, *Cancer pagurus,* are better appreciated with a salad than attached to a big toe.

Octopuses and squids

Stories of giant octopuses that seize men in their writhing arms and drag them down into the ocean abysses are common currency in sensational literature. What happens to the man is not always clear; sometimes he is rescued in the nick of time but otherwise we must assume that he is consumed by the octopus at its leisure. It makes a great story and I will not go on record as saying that it is impossible – only that it is unlikely.

The largest octopus ever caught was 28 feet from tip to tip of the arms when spread out. This sounds large, but the body of the specimen was only 1 foot across. Such big examples are usually to be found in rather deep water and not in the areas frequented by ordinary swimmers. A scuba diver might meet one if he were exploring a sunken wreck, but it would most likely retreat from him into whatever recess it had chosen as its lair.

Octopuses are shy creatures which hurry away at man's approach rather than attack him. They are extremely interesting creatures, too, and rather likeable to those who get to know them. Many of their activities remind us again and again of vertebrate animals and they exhibit a good deal more personality and awareness than some of the so-called higher groups. They represent a peak of development in a line of evolution which, though quite different from ours, has endowed them with features akin to our own. Their eyes, for example, are astonishingly similar to ours in structure and function, yet they have come about quite independently and are developed in a different way. It is sometimes difficult to remember that these are molluscs, related to mussels that grow on harbour piles and the snails that perforate the lettuces in our gardens. Yet fossils, and a few surviving intermediate forms, show that they were once creatures living in a shell and that, along with their relatives the cuttlefishes and squids, they have discarded the sheltered life for a more adventurous, swashbuckling career. They are given a class to themselves, the Cephalopoda. This name refers to the fact that the 'feet', which we usually call arms or tentacles, spring directly from the head and surround the mouth.

In the octopus there are, as the name implies, eight arms, more or less of the same length, usually with two rows of suckers along the underside of each. The control which the animal has over these arms is wonderful. Every sucker can be applied or released in the most sensitive fashion and the very tips of the arms, which are often quite finely drawn out, can be used with a finesse that would do credit to the fingers of a pianist. Between the arms, and varying in extent in different species, there is sometimes a web which serves as a blanket to be thrown over prey or as a shield for the eggs.

A male octopus has a special tip to one of his arms (called the hectocotylus) in which he carries his sperm. When he meets a female he thrusts it into her mantle and leaves it there. She may carry the sperm around for a long time before using it to fertilize her eggs. The female octopus is a very good mother. She lays her eggs – in groups, clusters or strings according to the species – attached to an overhanging wall of

Acute observation of marine life is shown in this splendid mosaic from Pompeii, now in the National Museum at Naples. A number of the animals mentioned in this book – octopus, squid, small sharks (dogfish), moray eel, electric ray – are clearly shown.

45

The suckers on the arms of the octopus are flat discs. In most species there are two rows on each arm.

rock or under the roof of a small cave and there she remains on guard, constantly cleaning them. It is here that the perfect control of the ends of her arms is most apparent, for she is continually fussing and finicking with each egg to ensure that it shall not have a blemish upon it. Now and again she will exhale a current of water from her siphon to wash away any debris.

If you approach her at this time she will turn with her back to the eggs and spread her arms in a dramatic gesture; the web hides her body and the eggs, and in its centre the parrot-like jaws confront you. These jaws are horny and rather like those of a parrot put on the wrong way up, with the lower jaw overlapping the upper. They are proportionately rather small, but well enough suited for their purpose.

An octopus feeds by seizing and smothering its prey – such as a crab – with its arms and biting a small hole through which it injects its poisonous saliva into the flesh. The flesh is thereby liquefied and can be sucked out. This would be an uncomfortable thing to happen to a skin-diver but I doubt if it ever has. Even the largest octopus will decamp at the approach of man, usually by scrambling rapidly over the rocks: there are times when perhaps the word 'foot' is after all more appropriate than 'arm', for an octopus in a hurry often seems to be running on eight legs. If hard pressed it will become jet-propelled by discharging water from the siphon under the head and shoot backwards. It can also do a disappearing act in two ways. Firstly, it can change colour suddenly. An animal of dark browns and greys is being stalked by a predator when, presto, it is not there; in its place is a pale thing of yellow and pink, and while the predator is adjusting its senses to the new image the prey has quietly slipped away. Secondly, when really alarmed the octopus can discharge its ink-sac, sending out a smoke-screen very much larger than itself, which by its sudden appearance and menacing increase in volume will confound the enemy while the octopus retires to some more hospitable spot.

There is really only one octopus that can be considered a serious danger to man – the most beautiful of all of them and one of the smallest, found on coasts in the neighbourhood of the Great Barrier Reef. This little menace, *Octopus maculosus*, is only a few inches in span from arm-tip to arm-tip and tends to frequent very shallow water. Sometimes it gets left upon the wet sand and is so attractive that beachcombers are tempted to pick it up. It has a variegated patchwork of rich browns and fawns on which are numerous shining blue spots and rings, the latter giving it the popular name of Blue-ringed Octopus. The whole effect is jewel-like, but anyone handling it is in peril, for a bite almost certainly means death. The saliva of this species is exceedingly virulent and no antidote is known. The most recently reported case was that of a man walking in the foam at the edge of the surf at Shoalhaven Harbour, New South Wales. He stepped upon a Blue-ringed Octopus and was bitten upon the big toe. After that he lived for less than five minutes.

There is another octopus that, while not so deadly as the Blue-ringed, is able to make itself painful to handle. This is the Blanket Octopus (*Tremoctopus*) which, when young, deliberately collects pieces of the tentacles of the Portuguese Man-of-war and places them along the underside of its arms. These serve not only as a protection but also to paralyze the small crustaceans that form its food. Pieces that have discharged all the nematocysts are discarded and replaced. This remarkable habit might well be claimed as a form of tool-using. When the octopus gets big enough to do without them, all the pieces of tentacles are jettisoned. Obviously it is as dangerous to handle a young Blanket Octopus as to touch *Physalia* itself.

If the size and habits of the octopus have been exaggerated, those of its relatives the Giant Squids (*Architeuthis*) have not. There has been some confusion between the two in early works, for old prints show the legendary Kraken as an octopus-like creature whereas the accounts indicate that it must have been a giant squid.

There is no doubt some truth in the Kraken stories. A considerable amount of evidence from parts of squids obtained at various times shows that *Architeuthis* grows very large indeed. The longest arm actually measured and recorded was 45 feet long, 2 feet in diameter at its wider end and had suckers at that end 'as big as a plate'. This was one of the eight arms; a squid has also two much longer members – the tentacles – with expanded, sucker-bearing blades at the ends for catching prey. Comparison of these measurements with the proportions

A Giant Squid *(Architeuthis)* washed up on the coast of Norway in an unusually intact condition. About 9 feet long from mouth to tip of tail and with tentacles 14 feet long, it is quite a small specimen of its kind. It is useful in that it shows the proportions whereby the sizes of larger ones can be judged from parts obtained from whales.

Above The suckers on the arms and tentacles of the squid are much more formidable than those of the octopus. They are movable on short stalks, and around the rim are teeth which hook into the skin of the prey. The photograph is of the leaf-shaped expansion at the end of one of the long tentacles.

known from smaller whole ones that are occasionally washed ashore, shows the entire animal to have been well over 100 feet in length.

Such an animal might weigh about 150 tons and if it seized the rigging of a small ship of early times it might well capsize it. It might do this if it were to take the ship to be a Sperm Whale. From many accounts it is clear that in the immense spaces of the oceans a continual war is being waged between Giant Squids and Sperm Whales. Squids form a large part of the diet of the whales but a large squid is often difficult to master. The long, narrow, lower jaw of the Sperm Whale seems to be well adapted for chopping off the arms – the large arm quoted above was obtained from a captured whale. Some of the reports of the 'sea-serpent' having a large body with humps and a long neck with a small head sprouting from it, suggest to me a Sperm Whale having difficulty with an extra large tentacle of a squid.

The skin of a Sperm Whale usually carries the characteristic round scars made by the suckers of squids, giving a clue to the titanic battles that must be fought out far below the surface. Both whale and squid can descend to considerable depths, though the whale must come up for air from time to time. It is interesting to speculate how many may have been drowned by large squids. The scars are made by hooks which are set round the rim of each sucker and dig like a cat's claws into the skin. When removed they take away a disc of skin and flesh, leaving a wound the size of the sucker. Some of the scars found on captured whales, when compared with the suckers on the largest arm mentioned earlier, show that there must be squids at least as long as 200 feet. Theoretically, there is hardly any limit to the size an animal can grow in the sea because of the physical characteristics of water, whereas the size of land animals is limited by a vicious circle of weight-muscle-weight.

The squid in its turn seems to feed on young whales, for several records have described brief appearances of great arms embracing a struggling Sperm Whale. The attacks on ships also indicate that the predation is a two-way affair. Even ships of today can be attacked, as shown by the interesting reports from the tanker *Brunswick* (15,000 tons) which, possibly because its route was more oceanic than most others, was assaulted by squids on three occasions. When this ship was travelling at 12 knots between Hawaii and Samoa, a large squid came after it at an estimated speed of 20 to 25 knots until it was running parallel at about 50 yards away. Then it turned and attacked the hull, trying to get a grip on the smooth sides about a third of the ship's length from the bow. When it found that it could not hold the ship, it drifted off and was cut to pieces by the propellors.

Unlike the octopus, the squid is a free-swimming, swift creature, as the foregoing account attests. The body is conical or cigar-shaped with a broad triangular fin on each side at the rear – or perhaps we should say the front end, for it swims 'backwards' with the head and arms trailing when moving at speed. It can, however, move forward by means of the fins, which also provide manoeuvrability in close encounters. Like the octopus it has parrot-like, horny jaws which often give further proof of enormous specimens, for some of the beaks found inside Sperm Whales are far larger than those of any examples that have been measured. Around the jaws are the eight arms with suckers set on short stalks so that they are more mobile than those of the octopus. In addition there are the two very much longer appendages, called tentacles to distinguish them from the arms. Beneath the head is a siphon through which a powerful jet of water can be thrust to drive the animal, tail first, at speed through the water. The eyes are very large, as often found in animals that move in fairly deep water and come to the surface at night. The squid, in fact, is well equipped to chase and capture its prey in the open sea and takes whatever it can find, including man if special circumstances bring him into its habitat.

For example, a Danish ship off West Africa was having its sides cleaned in the usual way by men sitting on 'cradles' formed of planks hung over the rail, when below them appeared a giant squid. Two men were seized, cradle and all, and dragged under water at once. A third man ran up the rigging but as he went a great arm, estimated at 35 feet long, reached up and seized him. Crew members on deck came to the rescue with hatchets and lopped off 25 feet of the arm, which remained dangling in the rigging. The man, mutilated by the hooked suckers, was extricated but died raving the same night.

War provides other occasions for the meeting between squid and man, by ditching aircraft or sinking ships in mid-ocean. No doubt many

go unrecorded but one at least is well documented. During the Second World War, on March 25, 1941, H.M.S. *Britannia* was sunk in the middle of the tropical Atlantic. Of the crew, twelve men were left adrift on a raft so small that they had to take turns hanging on to it in the water. One night one of them was seized by a large squid and dragged below, never to be seen again. Not long afterwards a tentacle attached itself to another man, Lieutenant R. E. G. Cox, who succeeded in freeing himself from it. As it left it took off discs of skin and flesh about 1¼ inches in diameter, indicating a squid about 23 feet long. The scars were examined and described two years later by Dr J. L. Cloudsley-Thompson, a well-known biologist.

There are, of course, many species of squids, some of which are quite small and make excellent eating in a ristorante beside the Bay of Naples. The really big ones are known to us only by an odd carcase cast up during a storm or an arm taken from the maw of a captured whale. Very rarely has a complete specimen of even a medium-sized *Architeuthis* been found and we have to reconstruct the largest by means of the bits and pieces and the various clues already described. Live examples are never seen close to shore.

For those unlucky enough to be dumped by an aircraft or ship-wrecked in mid-ocean there is no doubt a real danger of being held in eight clinging and very painful arms, nipped by a strong beak and dissolved out of their skins.

Far left The prettiest and most dangerous of the octopuses is also one of the smallest—the Blue-ringed Octopus, *Octopus maculosa.*

Above The octopus is the most highly developed of the molluscs and rival to the mammals in intelligence.

Left Eggs of the octopus suspended from an overhanging rock. The dark spots are the eyes of the developing embryos.

51

Starfish, sea urchins and sea cucumbers

The familiar starfish – or better, sea stars, for they are not fish – the prickly sea urchins, and the slug-like sea cucumbers that are dried and used as *bêche-de-mer* or trepang in the East, are all members of the great assemblage called Echinodermata (a Greek-derived name meaning 'prickly skinned'). The radiating structure shown by most of them and their comparative immobility creates an impression of creatures as lowly as the anemones and jellyfish, but in fact they seem to be more highly evolved. Study of their development from the egg yields the surprising information that they belong to the stock from which the chordates – the forerunners of the vertebrates – emerged. But for a twist in the evolutionary process a sea urchin might well have been sitting in

A close view of an arm of the Crown-of-thorns showing the tube feet.

your chair – but looking like you. The sea cucumbers even seem to have changed their mind too late, for during their development they begin as two-sided larvae, then acquire a radial symmetry like the others, but go on to adopt a secondary bilateral symmetry, becoming two-sided animals again.

However, we are here concerned with the fact that some of these interesting and often beautiful creatures can be dangerous. Those that are edible are often poisonous to eat at certain times of the year; others are able to inject poison by means of stings.

The sea stars need not occupy much space, for there is only one species that is really venomous and that is the Crown-of-thorns, *Acanthaster planci*, which has in recent years gained notoriety by indulging in its own population explosion, resulting in the destruction of large areas of coral reef. Its favourite food seems to be the coral polyps, whose stinging threads are powerless against it, while its armour of massive spines and its poisonous defences make it an unlikely prey for anything else. Moreover it is large, growing to about 2 feet across. It has from thirteen to sixteen arms which, by the way, are not limbs but extensions of the body in all directions. A starfish has no front or rear but moves in the direction of whichever arm receives the most attractive stimulus. The arms have a large number of tube-feet on their underside which are marvellously co-ordinated by a simple nervous system and which push the animal wherever it elects to go. The mouth is at the centre underneath, but a sea star does not bite or masticate its food; instead it pushes all or part of its stomach out through the mouth to invest the prey, then proceeds to digest it outside, where there is much more room for the job.

The Crown-of-thorns gets its name from the large, sharp spines, often up to 3 inches in length, with which it is covered. They are ensheathed in thin skin containing venom-secreting cells. It is difficult to handle these without getting pricked and the result is a very painful wound that becomes inflamed and swells, leaving the victim numb and

Sea cucumbers have the curious habit of ejecting their viscera when alarmed.

more or less paralysed, and continually vomiting. Many other sea stars have poisonous properties but they are directed against other marine animals and are not known to bother man.

With sea urchins it is different, for in various parts of the world their ripe ovaries are considered a delicacy by the local population. In Britain the edible sea urchin is *Echinus esculenta*; in the Mediterranean the 'frutta di mare' is *Paracentrotus lividus*; in the West Indies the 'sea egg' is *Tripneustes ventricosus*. The ovaries are eaten either raw or cooked, but it is advisable to obtain information from the local people before trying them, for taken at the wrong time they can be very upsetting to the inner workings – nausea, vomiting, stomach-ache, diarrhoea and bad headaches are among the usual symptoms.

However, many sea urchins can be poisonous in quite a different way. A sea urchin is, in effect, a five-pointed sea star that has disposed of its upper skin and bent its arms over its back to cover itself. The tips of the arms meet above so that they form a dome; the mouth remains underneath. The tube-feet thus form five radiating series around the resulting globe, the pattern of which can be seen on the empty dried specimens sold as curios or on fossils found on the beach. The urchin did not really come about like this, but it gives the general idea.

The skin is hardened with limey plates to form a shell or 'test' and in life it is covered with a large number of movable spines which usually give the impression of a small hedgehog. Mostly these spines are solid and short, but in some they may be much modified – very large, stout and few like those of the Slate-pencil Urchin, or long and thin like the diadem urchins.

In tropical waters the diadems particularly are a menace, for they are very numerous and it is difficult to avoid coming against them when skin-diving or wading. They take their name from the Black Long-spined Urchin, *Diadema setosum*, which has a shining blue spot on each of the five plates on the back, giving the impression, from above, of a diadem of gleaming jewels. But there are others – the Sea Needle *D. antillarum* of the Caribbean and the Needle-spined Urchin *D. savignyi* of the Indo-Pacific.

The spines of all these are very slender and can reach a length of 1 foot on an animal only 3 inches across; they are hollow and extremely sharp. What makes them so unpleasant is that they can pierce not only the skin but a diving suit or a shoe and are so brittle that they then break off, the ends remaining imbedded in the flesh. They produce intense pain – far more than a mere puncture would cause – and it is evident that the hollow space in each spine is filled with poison, though no specific venom has yet been found. Moreover, a bad sting will result in the symptoms usually associated with echinoderm toxica-tion – inflammation, swelling, aching, numbness, partial paralysis of the legs, irregular pulse and so on. The spines also introduce a violet-coloured fluid into the wound which remains for several days, although the other symptoms are gone in a few hours provided there is no secondary infection.

If the spines are deeply imbedded they will have to be surgically removed to avoid possible complications, but superficial pieces can be picked out with tweezers. Any pieces remaining under the skin are best dealt with by pounding the affected area with a flat stone – this breaks

The Crown-of-thorns, *Acanthaster planci*.

54

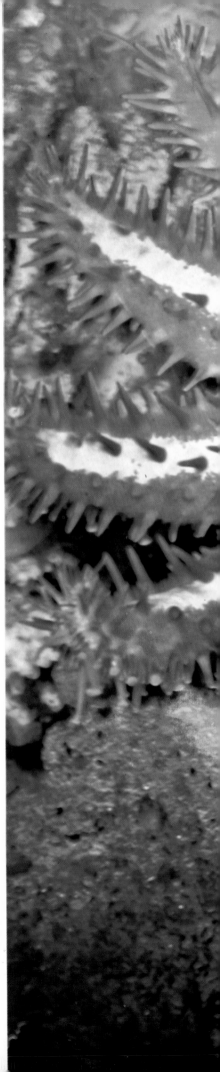

them up, aiding their absorption by the tissues. Oddly enough I have found that this hammering on the skin helps to reduce the pain – perhaps by diluting the venom in the slight contusion caused.

Large numbers of these urchins are usually to be found just below the tide mark in tropical waters, generally lying fairly close or even sitting in pits in the rock or coral. The side towards the sunlight usually has longer spines than that in the shadow. Fortunately they are fairly conspicuous as a rule, but it is terribly easy to knock against the fine tips if one is engrossed in watching something else or being pulled about by the tide.

Members of the genus *Echinothrix*, belonging to the same family, are equally dangerous. *E. calamaris* of Malaya and the East Indies comes in an assortment of bright colours. *E. diadema* of the Australian region is dark in colour but the spines are usually shorter than in *Diadema* proper. Young specimens of all the diadem urchins have the spines banded with black and buff.

Another Australian genus, *Centrostephanus*, has spines that look stout and strong but are in fact fragile, thin shells. It is very dangerous to handle these for they break almost at a touch, inflicting painful wounds that take a long time to heal.

Even more dangerous to handle is *Asthenosoma varium* of the Indo-Pacific, which grows to about 6 inches across. This is one of the short-spined urchins, but certain of the spines on the upper surface have their sharp tips encased in a venomous sheath. It often gets into the nets of fishermen, who treat it with the greatest respect until it has been successfully disentangled, after which they smash it up.

But this is not all. Sea urchins have, among the spines, interesting structures called pedicellariae, which are used for defence, for cleaning the test, or for obtaining food. A pedicellaria when expanded looks rather like a little flower on a slender stalk, and in some species it is likely to be brightly coloured like a flower. Seen more closely it proves to be an equilateral triangle formed largely of three 'petals' radiating from the centre. At the tip of each petal, at each corner of the triangle, is a fang-like claw. The petal itself is composed of a broad venom-sac from which runs a central duct to the fang. At the base of each duct, near the centre of the 'flower', is a dark muscle.

If anything touches the centre of this structure the muscles bring the 'petals' together to close the flower and the three fangs dig into whatever has provided the stimulus. The fangs are perforated so that the poison in the ducts is injected. If the object is lifeless the pedicellaria will pass it on to another and release it so that it is moved over the surface and dropped as part of the cleaning routine; but if the object is living it is gripped until the venom does its work and movement ceases, even though the stalk may be ripped away from the shell. A pedicellaria can go on functioning for some time independently of the urchin.

It is difficult to know whether to say a pedicellaria stings or bites. Whichever it may be, a number of sea urchins are capable of doing it to humans. To avoid a tedious list of scientific names (for few of these have vernacular names and if they have they differ from one place to another) only the worst need be mentioned, with the comment that the others give similar results on a milder level. (No guarantee is offered for the mildness, however.)

Toxopneustes pileolus is the one to be pilloried. It is from the Indo-Pacific, where so many poisonous things abound, and is not particularly

Upper The tropical sea urchin *Toxopneustes pileolus* has large, flower-like pedicellariae that project beyond the spines.

Lower Close-up of the pedicellariae of *Toxopneustes*. A claw at each corner of the triangle injects poison into the prey.

Following pages The young of long-spined sea urchins of the genera *Diadema* and *Echinothrix* have banded spines as in this photograph. In time the spines become longer and turn black.

large or spectacular – just an ordinary urchin with short, solid spines. But it has exceptionally large pedicellariae that push up well beyond the spines and spread their flower-like jaws in an assortment of pretty colours.

If you pick up this little flowery thing you will have difficulty in putting it down again, because numerous tiny fangs will have jabbed into your hand, hanging on. It will seem very important to put it down because it will hurt very much indeed. It will make you feel faint and soon a general weakness and numbness will occur. If you are fortunate the pain will last for an hour; weakness or paralysis may remain for several hours. With bad luck the paralysis will be much worse; you will gasp for breath, your heart will stop and when the real flowers arrive you won't see them. *Toxopneustes* poison acts directly on the heart.

The only other echinoderms that need be mentioned are the Holothuria or sea cucumbers, some of which have a special poison of their own called (you'll never guess) holothurin. There are many species from most parts of the world and sometimes they are abundant.

The wide, sandy flats along the northern coast of the Somali Republic are littered with *Holothuria scabra* looking very much like king-size garden slugs at first sight and appearing to be pretty lifeless. Actually they are taking in large quantities of the sand at one end, where some short tentacles surround a mouth, and ejecting it from the other end, any nourishing material having been extracted on the way through. On wading over the flats as one often must, since at low tide the water lies too shallow for a boat to come within half a mile of shore, it is necessary to walk over a carpet of these sea-cucumbers. It is quite safe to do this and one may pick them up gently and cast them aside. Fooling about with them, however, causes small scratches from the numerous minute granules of lime in the leathery skin and the toxin may then cause dermatitis. The eyes should never be rubbed by hands that have touched Holothuria or blindness may follow.

At Zeila in the Somali Republic I used to watch a man collect these animals, remove their innards, and boil them. This done he would dig a large hole in dry sand and fill it with layers of them, with salt packed between each layer. The salt and sand together dehydrated the sea cucumbers (sometimes the drying is achieved by smoking) and they were then *bêche-de-mer*, which he exported to the East for use in curries. In Malaya the name for this delicacy is trepang. At a later time I would look at the heaps in the markets at Kuala Lumpur or Singapore and wonder if they came from Zeila, though of course they are collected at many other places.

Other species are utilized in much the same way elsewhere and some have proved to be poisonous when eaten, perhaps through incorrect preparation beforehand. Usually holothurin is a far greater danger to fish than to man. Sea cucumbers and fish cannot be kept together in the same tank, except in the odd case of the fish *Carapus* that is able to live inside the holothurian without harm, apparently immune to the toxin.

Certain holothurians are known as 'cotton-spinners' from their extraordinary habit of ejecting long, viscous threads to entangle any crab or other animal that annoys them. They can go even further and outdo the performance of the sea stars mentioned earlier – they not only turn the stomach inside out but hurl it along with other viscera at their aggressor, moving off to grow a new set elsewhere. What might be called an empty victory.

Sharks and other killers

Of all the dangers, real or imaginary, that exist in the sea, attack by a shark is the one that most easily captures the imagination and is the most publicized. The idea of a shark as a creature that swallows you or bites pieces from you is crystallized in the use of the word to denote a human predator such as a rapacious landlord or a commercial profiteer.

Human beings have been badly bitten by sharks and in a few cases, it seems, even swallowed completely. No doubt the number of such occurrences will multiply with the increasing migration of thousands of holiday-makers to the regions in which sharks abound. Nevertheless it is quite erroneous to suppose that these creatures are prowling around looking for humans as prey. As earlier pointed out, man does not belong to the sea; he is the animal a shark might least expect to meet and when it does its reaction is usually either fear or curiosity.

Sharks are very interesting creatures for those who can overcome irrational prejudice. Generally regarded as fish, they are so different from the kind of fish we commonly see on the market such as herring, cod, plaice or salmon that I prefer to call them selachians. Not only do they show many anatomical differences from the true fishes but their mode of reproduction and their basic chemical make-up are also very different.

Their history as recorded by fossils goes back at least to Devonian times, some three hundred million years ago, and in all that time they have changed very little. They are so perfectly adapted both physiologically and structurally for the life they lead that there has been no need for change. It could be argued that it is those groups that are less well organized that must keep trying this and trying that in an endeavour to cope with a varying environment – perhaps that is why there are some twenty thousand kinds of true fishes but only about two hundred and fifty kinds of sharks.

Most of the sharks are small and quite harmless to man. Those who, like myself, enjoy the 'huss', 'flake' or 'rock salmon' served in many fish restaurants are eating a small shark – usually the Spur Dog,

A catch of sharks being cut up on the beach. In the foreground is a fine specimen of the Black-tipped Shark, *Carcharhinus sorrah*.

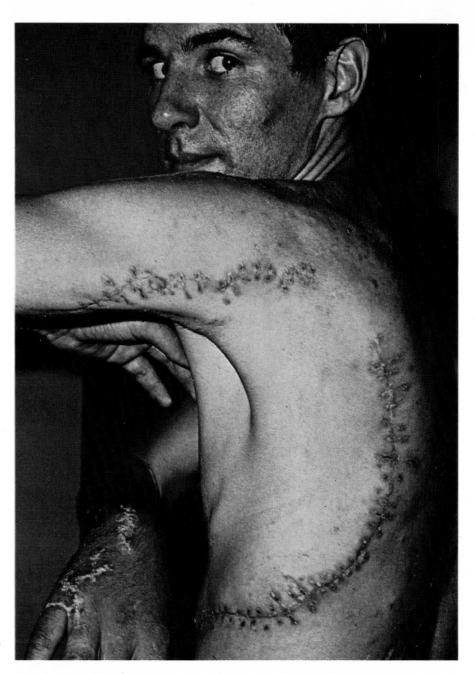

After being bitten by a shark, this diver will carry scars for life.

Squalus acanthias, but sometimes the Spotted Dogfish, *Scyliorhinus stellaris*. The flesh of these little selachians is among the best to be eaten – soft and sweet and, in terms of calories, ranking only below the salmon and herring in nutritive value. It has, moreover, the advantage of being without sharp bones, for the sharks have never developed the hard skeleton that supports the muscles of true fish.

The skeleton of a shark is composed almost entirely of cartilage (gristle) and is comparatively simple – a box-like skull with the jaws and gill arches suspended underneath, a central supporting rod or 'back-bone' made up of a series of small drums to give flexibility, and some gristly supports for the fins. The fins themselves contain horny fibres that keep them rigid; they do not fold down like those of fish.

Sharks are usually recognizable at a glance by reason of the row of gill slits on each side of the head (in a fish the gills are covered by plates of bone) and by the shape of the tail, which is turned up to carry the long upper part of the caudal fin, the lower lobe being usually very

Portrait of the Great White Shark, *Carcharodon carcharias,* largest and most aggressive of the so-called man-eaters.

much smaller. Only in the fast-swimming mackerel sharks and one or two others does the tail fin approach a symmetrical shape.

The characteristic roughness of shark skin, known as shagreen, is due to numerous, small, very hard structures called denticles. These 'little teeth' are well named for they are generally considered to be the fore-runners of all teeth. If an embryo shark is examined it will be found that the denticles are formed early and that they extend into the mouth; later the jaws and lips develop in such a way as to separate those out-side from those inside and the latter grow much larger to become teeth.

It is an odd thought that our own teeth, that give us so much trouble when we are getting them, when we have got them and when we have to get rid of them, should have begun aeons ago as prickles on the skin of a shark. What is more, a shark does not have dental trouble. The teeth are not set in sockets from which it is difficult to extract them; they are only lightly set on the edge of the jaw so that when worn or broken by violent use they can be shed easily and replaced; behind the front row is always rank upon rank of other teeth waiting to move into first place. Evolution, you can see, is not always progress. Sharks have the laugh on us in this and other respects. They came here long before us and I suspect they will continue without much change long after we are extinct.

The fact that the teeth of a shark come out so easily and are some-times so curiously brittle that they will break against a human bone often provides the only way of knowing which species has been responsible for an attack. There are subtle differences in the shape of the teeth from one species to another so that it is sometimes possible to identify the shark by means of a single tooth or even a piece of tooth.

The number of kinds of shark that warrant inclusion in this book is really very small. The great majority of species are either too small, too timid or too far beyond reach to be of concern to any human entering the water. Quite a few of them inhabit very deep water and are seen only by fishermen on long-distance trawlers, who throw them back as of no commercial value; these are usually dark brown or black in colour, often with luminous organs to light their way in the gloom of the ocean deeps.

At the other end of the scale, the two largest kinds of shark, the Whale Shark, *Rhincodon typus*, and the Basking Shark, *Cetorhinus maximus*, are also quite harmless for they feed on the plankton, the mass of small floating life that exists in stupendous quantities in the oceans. Indeed, in these cases it is man who is a danger to the sharks, for from time immemorial the Basking Shark has been hunted for its oil off the western coasts of Britain and although this has lately abated new fisheries have developed to supply a demand for another substance, squalene, used in cosmetics. The Whale Shark, though not so persecuted, is a blundering fellow liable to get in the way of ships and be rammed or cut up by the propellers, or to get tangled in fishermen's nets and killed as a nuisance.

Of the remainder, those that come within the ken of the sportsman or holiday-maker, only a few can be marked with certainty as a potential danger – about twenty-five kinds according to my list or just a tenth of the total number of species. Not that anyone except an ichthyologist is likely to wait around to ascertain whether the grey shape coming towards him is dangerous or harmless. For most people a shark is a shark and a snake is a snake and at first sign of either they will retreat

Left One of the largest sharks, the Basking Shark, is quite harmless to man. It feeds by moving through the water with its mouth open as in this picture. Small organisms are strained from the water by the large gills which are visible inside the mouth.

Right Carcharhinid sharks often move along coasts in shoals.

at full speed or lash out with the nearest offensive weapon. And who can blame them?

With snakes particularly there is some justification, because some of the harmless ones have the confusing habit of resembling the poisonous ones. Moreover there are about two hundred and fifty species of poisonous snakes and, although this is a small percentage of the total number, they are sometimes common enough as individuals to be a constant threat. They account for about thirty-five thousand deaths throughout the world each year.

Sharks, on the other hand, are involved in only fifty to a hundred incidents each year, only a few of them fatal. It is quite likely, of course, that a good many more have not been recorded because the victim did not survive to tell the story, but even so we all face greater peril several times a day when we try to cross a modern road.

The chances against being attacked by a shark are about thirty million to one, but if the one happens to be you all the rest will suddenly seem unimportant. It has to be admitted that a bite from a shark is a very messy and horrible business and that the general fear of these animals is not by any means groundless.

Recently, as this book was in preparation, John Fairfax with his lady companion Sylvia Cook, rowed a boat across the Pacific Ocean. It took them almost exactly a year, but so far from being an exciting adventure it seems to have been a pretty dull and uneventful voyage except for one notable incident. When about 200 miles from New Caledonia Mr Fairfax was bitten by a shark. He lost about 12 inches of skin from his arm and Miss Cook had the task of staunching a copious flow of blood. This information I have garnered from the newspapers, for sharks make better headlines than dogged oarsmen. But I also gather that this was no wanton attack by a merciless monster. John Fairfax himself stated that the shark was not to blame.

What happened, it seems, was that Fairfax had caught a fish and was

bringing it to the side when the shark took a bite at it. Reasonably annoyed at this the fisherman jabbed at the shark which, equally reasonably, retaliated as many a dog would have done.

This is the most recent example of a type of encounter that occurs quite often among the records of 'shark attacks'. It is a type that will no doubt become more frequent now that large numbers of people with aqualungs and arboletes are invading the habitat of the sharks unless the correct lesson is drawn from the contents of this chapter.

About a third of the 'shark attacks' recorded up to the present time would be better described as 'shark retaliations'. A few of them have occurred at the side or even on the deck of a vessel when the shark was captured. Many others have taken place in the water as a result of foolhardy behaviour by swimmers and divers. It is wise to treat sharks with great respect when meeting them in their own element. In any kind of contest the odds are in favour of the shark, for it is perfectly adapted for movement in the water and can easily outpace and outmanoeuvre the most confident human swimmer.

Quite a number of species of sharks, particularly those of the family Carcharhinidae, sometimes called cub sharks, exhibit behaviour reminiscent of wild dogs or wolves. It is not really surprising that names like 'dogfish' or 'hound' have been given to some of them. An unusual object such as a skin diver arouses the curiosity of one of these and it moves round in a wide circle to investigate. It is nervous and at this stage any alarming phenomenon will cause it to make off at high speed. Some undersea explorers have recommended sudden movements to frighten it off. This is all very well if you are quite sure what species you are dealing with, but some kinds of shark are *attracted* by a commotion in the water. The trick of releasing a sudden gush of air bubbles seems more effective as it startles the senses of the animal. The best thing to do is to leave the water as soon as a shark is sighted, but this too has its dangers; for in clambering into a boat the shark is presented, not with a large and alarming foreign body, but with a little waggling limb at the surface that appears about the size of its usual prey and is very tempting.

The appearance of a shark therefore, under any circumstances, is a nuisance to a skin diver and causes a good deal of misgiving. Often it is better to stay around hoping the creature will decide you are not a necessary part of his life. His curiosity may cause him to move round in circles of decreasing diameter. If he moves in for a closer look some authorities recommend meeting him face to face and hitting him on the nose. This might have the desired effect of causing him to decamp, but I wouldn't care to bet on it. He may just as well retaliate, in which case you are in trouble. If you manage to leave the water you may be minus something you valued, but the smell of your blood may bring others to the scene and you will then be posted as missing.

Sharks can smell blood in the water from an astonishing distance and they immediately move toward the source of it. Again like dogs or wolves, the timid individuals become quite fearless when they are in a pack. During recent wars numerous men have been lost through being cast into tropical waters with bleeding wounds that rallied the sharks.

When in such a pack the creatures sometimes go into a frenzy, dashing around, leaping and rolling, biting at anything including each other. Once off the Socotra Islands I saw a great shoal of little horse mackerel packed in a tight school, for around and below them were

One of the more dangerous cub sharks, *Carcharhinus leucas,* taking a Weakfish suspended as bait at the surface.

Head of the Sand Shark, *Carcharias taurus,* showing the slender, awl-like grasping teeth and the folds at the corner of the mouth that give it a permanent smile. Unlike its Old-world cousins, this American species seems to be peacable.

tuna taking toll of those on the outside. Then suddenly the sharks moved in and the sea boiled over an area of an acre or more. Great fins cleft the water around the shoals and the surface glittered with the leaping bodies of horse mackerel and tuna alike; but soon the sharks began hurling themselves above the surface too, flopping back at all angles and thrashing the water with their tails. The horse mackerel and tuna then seemed to disperse and I did not see them again, but the sharks kept up their frenzied rolling and leaping for some time afterwards. These sharks were of the cub shark family, as we found by catching some.

Sharks of this group are the ones the swimmer is most likely to meet in warm waters and the genus *Carcharhinus* has more species than any other selachian group. At present it is not quite certain how many species there are, for many of them look very much alike and can be distinguished only by close examination. With smaller animals this could be done in a museum by collecting specimens preserved in formalin or spirit, but with things the size of sharks this is difficult – the weight in transport, the size of receptacle required, the amount of preservative involved and the space needed for storage all discourage accumulation of comparative material. If a female with young is caught, advanced foetuses can be preserved because many of the distinguishing features will already be present. Sometimes such a female will give birth when brought on board ship, providing specimens of a size that can be bottled.

In recent years a number of dedicated research workers have been catching sharks at sea, measuring them, photographing them and collecting the jaws and teeth. The last procedure is most rewarding and anyone able to examine a dead shark under any circumstances should if possible take the jaws and dry them. A label – stating time and place, length of body, head and fins – should be tied to the jaws and they should then be sent to an important museum. This may enable an ichthyologist to name the species or use it as evidence in future research.

In this family Carcharhinidae and in some others the upper teeth are different from the lower and this is related to the way a shark bites – it does not as a rule take a clean snap. The lower teeth are fairly upright and pointed, but those in the upper jaw are usually broader and bent outwards so that one of their sides is facing obliquely downwards as a cutting edge. It is a knife and fork arrangement: the lower pointed teeth dig into the food and hold it in position while the head moves from side to side, shearing through the flesh as a breadknife cuts through a loaf. Thus, in those cases where an unfortunate person has provided a meal, there is often an awful, gaping hollow from which the mouthful has been taken and a narrow gash where the lower jaw has held the limb or the body as the case may be. Only when a very large shark has taken a bite big enough for the jaws to be brought together will the accessory wound be obliterated.

To bite in this way a shark has to turn up its nose and the longer this is the more difficult it will be to use the jaws in a frontal attack. It is hardly surprising, therefore, that the sharks most often doing damage to human beings are those with comparatively short, broadly rounded snouts. But this turning up of the nose is used by many of them as a threatening gesture.

However curious a shark may be about the intentions of an intruding human, it is also basically alarmed and in some situations alarm may be the overriding factor. With certain important reservations I believe that the majority of attacks by sharks are not for the purpose of obtaining food but are an attempt to drive away the intruder. We may compare again the behaviour of a dog, which does not bite the burglar in order to enjoy the meat but to drive off someone who should not be there and who therefore scares him. This kind of reaction works on the principle that attack is the best defence – and usually works very well.

We know all too little about the behaviour of sharks. Do they have any territorial ambitions, for instance? Certainly it seems that many kinds do not wander all over the sea, but tend to congregate in certain areas. This is why some optimistic fisheries for shark (for the skin and oil) have ended in failure. If the fishery is successful it soon catches the majority of sharks in that area, after which it is uneconomic to continue. Other sharks do not immediately migrate from their territories to occupy the depleted area; the few sharks that are left will breed, but it may take years before the population is of a size to encourage another fishery.

Just what are the conditions that determine the presence of sharks in large numbers is not really known, though as most sharks are fish eaters it may be assumed that an abundance of fish is an important factor. In the Gulf of Aden, where I was involved in a survey of the fisheries for several years, sharks were fairly localized. The Arabs of Bir Ali on the southern coast of Arabia have from time immemorial been culling the shark population of the Gulf, exporting salted meat, skins and liver oil to markets elsewhere. But they do not get many sharks on the Arabian side – they go across to the Somali coast where sharks are indeed plentiful. The set of the currents has something to do with this, for certain fishes such as tuna are far more frequent on that coast and they are most attractive to the larger sharks. Longlines set to catch tuna often came in with just the head of the fish, the rest having been bitten off, or with the shark itself, tuna and hook still in its gullet.

On the Australian and some other coasts sharks seem to be more frequently encountered at river mouths, perhaps because the silt brought into the sea at such points supports a food chain at the apex of which the shark sits.

Whatever the reason for the patchiness of distribution, however, I do not think an individual shark marks out a territory for itself and mate. Some carcharhinid sharks, as already noted, hunt in parties and it may be that they patrol a particular area; they are also believed to congregate for breeding. It is the intruder on some such private occupation who is likely to be met with threatening behaviour or attack.

When scared of an unfamiliar object or creature, a cub shark turns up its nose. The mouth is thus brought to the forefront and, slightly opening, gives a sickly grin, displaying an array of teeth – for all the world like a dog snarling. If you stay to watch, its next move is to go stiff and arch its back – you would see the hackles rising if it had any. It next begins to wave the whole body, still stiffly, so that the head swings from side to side in anticipation of that movement that will operate on you like a breadknife. It is then moving forward to start the business, but if you have taken the hint you will not be there when it arrives. If it is with a party it will not follow you when you retreat but will return to its companions, having successfully defended them against a dangerous creature.

This fear reaction seems to be the basic explanation for the rogue shark that manifests itself occasionally off popular beaches at Florida, Natal and Australia, where the water is invaded by hordes of alien creatures, many of them with spear-guns. In some places the authorities

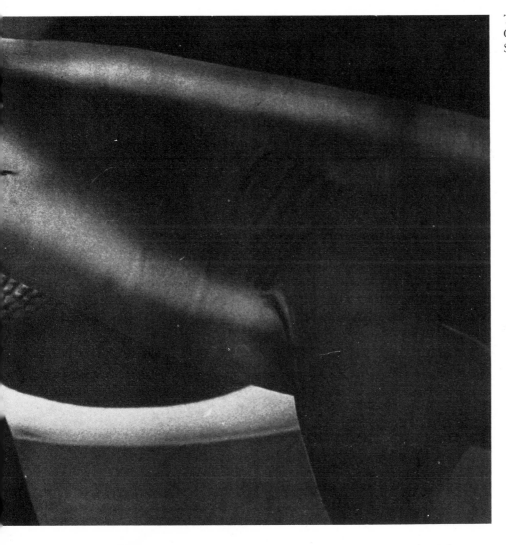

The Killer Whale, the Estuarine Crocodile and the Great White Shark.

have taken the trouble to erect fences to protect the sharks, but elsewhere one of them may be upset by a human who is more adventurous than the others and will do its attack routine. If the human tastes nice – and some of them do, Papuans tell me – the shark may get a compulsive urge to add more to its menu whenever opportunity arises. In a number of recorded cases there has been a series of attacks on swimmers within a few days; then a single shark has been caught and the trouble has ceased, showing that this one rogue with unusual tastes has been responsible.

Quite often an attack does not result in a bite at all but a slash, particularly from the long-snouted species which have more difficulty in bringing the mouth forward for a frontal assault. What they do is draw the lower jaw back out of the way, leaving the upper cutting teeth exposed, then override the enemy, swinging the head sideways for the breadknife cut. A number of the recorded cases are consistent with this behaviour.

A shark that objects to an intruder rarely bites or slashes more than once or twice; having made its point it departs, leaving him mutilated and shocked. It does not devour him because he is a foreign body, not the natural prey of any sea creature. If he remains there, however, the smell of his blood may bring others, perhaps of different species, for whom he will be an attractive bait. Anyone so injured must be removed from the water at once. There are some inspiringly heroic rescues recorded. It needs immense courage to swim out to a stricken person knowing that a shark is close at hand.

Yet curiously, rescuers are rarely if ever attacked; it appears as though the animosity of the shark is conditioned to the first objective, unless the appearance of more of the foreign bodies discourages it. Of the recorded cases, that of the crew of the *Comorin* is very striking. The southern part of the Red Sea is so heavily populated with sharks that it has been said it is impossible to die there by drowning. Yet when, way back in 1895, a man went overboard from the *Comorin*, a man went over with a lifebuoy to save him. Because the ship, disabled by damaged machinery, could not stop, it had to circle while a lifeboat was launched but the lifeboat upended, tipping the would-be rescuers into the sea. All these men were in the sea for four hours with sharks circling round them, yet not one was attacked. This story, among many others, is given in more detail by Paul Budker, to whose entertaining book I would refer anyone wishing to know more about these animals than the scope of the present work allows. His general attitude is that any shark should be treated with care as it is not possible to predict what it will do.

Occasionally a large shark not only tries to discourage a swimmer by biting or slashing but by shoving him as well. In a number of recorded cases the first intimation that he is *persona non grata* is a thump under the chest that lifts him vertically out of the water. As he shoots up his legs are vulnerable; either, as in an American case, he is seized by them and dragged under, never to be seen again, or, as in a South African case, both legs are bitten off. Such an amputation seems difficult to credit, but not long ago the bite of an 8 foot shark was scientifically tested and found to exert a pressure of three metric tons per square centimetre. No wonder steel wires and chains are sometimes bitten through.

The shoving technique itself can be very damaging to the skin, owing to the denticles with which the shark is covered: large areas of abrasion may result. Moreover, the rough edges of the rigid fins, even of a small shark, can cut human skin if the animal swims against it at speed.

A swimmer hardly ever sees the shark that attacks him – except perhaps as a great shadowy shape after he has already been struck. Curiously, in many cases this seems to give little pain, partly perhaps through being under water, mostly no doubt due to shock. Swimmers describe the bite as a 'thud' or 'sudden pressure' and often display a horrific awareness, like the tragic John Gibson at St Thomas in the Virgin Islands. His friend Miss Diana Waugh saw, too late, that he was in difficulties and bravely swam out to help him. The poor fellow had already lost a hand and was being eaten piece by piece, yet he called to

her to go back, explaining what was happening. She persisted, even though the shark followed, still biting great pieces out of its victim. When he was at last brought ashore he was of course dead. This is the kind of story that imprints itself on the mind as an example of the horror of a shark attack and the incredible courage it can summon up in the people concerned. The shark was caught next day, the hand and pieces of flesh still inside it; amazingly it turned out to be a Pacific species, the Galapagos Shark, previously unknown in the Atlantic. This shark, incidentally, is a particularly aggressive kind that made work in the sea practically impossible for an expedition to its domain in 1956; men, boats, equipment, everything was attacked. Nothing would drive these sharks away – they even ate a shark repellent that was being tried out!

No really reliable shark repellent has been found, though the US Navy has gone to a great deal of trouble to discover one. Some are found to work under certain conditions but not under others; some repel one species more than another. I doubt very much whether any universally successful substance or device is possible.

Fences to keep sharks away from bathing beaches are effective but costly. They need constant repair, although strangely enough they sometimes work even after great holes have rotted in them. I used to go through one barrier with ease though I never heard of a shark doing so. Possibly the fence in its early days conditions the animals to a particular beat that they maintain even when they could later deviate from it. Not that I really believe this, knowing how little they follow rules.

The Galapagos Shark mentioned above is one notable exception to my view that fear may motivate attacks and there are others. No general statement can be made that will apply to all species of sharks and no prediction can be made as to what even the best behaved specimen will do under unusual circumstances.

Although feeding mainly on crustacea from the sea bed, the Nurse Shark can be dangerous to swimmers if annoyed.

At Ghardaqa in the Red Sea Province of Egypt there is a biological station where much valuable research has been done. A fair-sized compound has been built in the sea, so that a variety of specimens can be confined in it while still getting the benefit of the natural water that flows through it. When I was there some years ago there were some huge animals in it – a big Sawfish, some rays and a member of a 'harmless' group of sharks called orectolobids or carpet sharks. Carpet sharks have small, close-set teeth and sensitive flaps round the mouth for locating molluscs, crabs and similar creatures, for they are bottom feeders.

This particular specimen of *Ginglymostoma ferrugineum* – sorry I have no simpler name for it – seemed a friendly old thing and if I climbed on its back it would swim slowly around like a patient donkey giving a child a ride round the paddock. It is blissful to be ignorant. Some years elapsed before I first heard of an attack by this species, or something closely allied, in Malaya, and learned that its American representative, *G. cirrhatum*, the Nurse Shark, is generally considered very dangerous. My Egyptian friend, thank goodness, had not read the rule book.

The Wobbegongs of Australia also belong to this family and may be considered inoffensive if unmolested in their own environment. All recorded attacks by them have been in retaliation. As long ago as 1789 one was caught during the settlement of Botany Bay and left on the ship's deck for two hours. This is really more than the most patient shark can stand, so when an officer's dog came too close the Wobbegong seized its leg, causing great indignation by its 'ferocity'. Another one bit a man in 1951 at Avalon in New South Wales, but in that case the swimmer had actually grabbed the creature. Another case, near Fremantle, Western Australia, occurred in 1960, when a diver speared a Wobbegong which promptly gripped his arm. The diver tried to prise open the jaws with his knife but when he found he could not he tried to kill the animal. This convinced the shark that he was not friendly, so when another diver came to the rescue the Wobbegong grabbed his posterior and was towed thereby to the boat (I mentioned that they were bottom feeders.)

In such cases my sympathy is all with the shark. I have little time for degenerates who take pleasure in killing things unnecessarily and none at all for spear fishers, who do more damage to an area in one season than ordinary fishermen can do in fifty years. Before the Second World War there were spots in the Mediterranean which were a paradise for an observer with a home-made pair of goggles and a pair of good lungs; now, since the invention of the aqualung and the spear gun those same places are submarine deserts. No animal in this book is as vicious as man and certainly none as despicable as the 'sportsman' who kills for his own amusement. However, I digress.

The point made earlier that sharks frequently attack as a response to fear is not by any means a rule. There are species that will attack and eat anything, familiar or not, when they are hungry, and some that kill wantonly, or so it seems to us, through sheer aggressiveness. The Galapagos Shark already mentioned is a case in point.

Of all the carcharhinid family, the most notorious is the Tiger Shark, *Galeocerdo cuvier*. Its reputation stems not, I think, from any actual excess of rapacity when compared with others but from the ferocious-sounding name. The Tiger Shark rarely exceeds 14 feet in length and is usually a good deal less; 10 feet is a common size. It gets its

A large carcharhinid shark swimming with a sucker fish, *Leptecheneis,* attached beneath it. The sucker on top of the head is actually a modified dorsal fin that creates a powerful vacuum by movement of the rays. The sucker fish is able to hitch for long distances and share the food of its host being careful to attach itself where the shark cannot bite it.

name not for its voracity but for the dark stripes across its side; they are quite prominent in young ones but get fainter with age. The teeth are quite different from those of other carcharhinids in several ways. Firstly, they are alike in both jaws, secondly the points are abruptly bent outwards so that the sides form a more or less continuous cutting edge, and thirdly the edges have notches in them, forming very coarse saw teeth. The tooth of a Tiger Shark is highly characteristic and recognizable at once. The whole dentition makes a very efficient biting apparatus, both jaws being able to saw with a sideways motion together. The Tiger Shark has a short, broadly rounded snout, which I have already suggested is a bad sign. In all respects it looks like a killer. But there is no need to single out the Tiger Shark above others. Although a number of undoubted cases of attack have been reported, my own view, on fairly close acquaintance with the animal, is that its reputation as a man-eater is rather exaggerated.

It is a scavenger, living close to the sea bed at most times and picking up anything it finds lying around. For this reason it is very likely to be found in harbours, where there is always plenty of refuse thrown out from ships' galleys or dumped by local fishermen. It will take pieces from any drowned person and if later a bone or two is found in its stomach it is proclaimed a man-eater. But apart from discarded fish,

pieces of meat and so on it picks up the most extraordinary things – bottles, old boots, rubber tyres, empty sacks, and cans of various kinds. It cannot digest these, nor pass them through its alimentary system; if they cause any discomfort, the shark pushes its stomach out through its mouth and tips the lot out (shades of those echinoderms we met earlier!)

Having said all this, however, it must also be stated that this shark takes live prey as well and has been undoubtedly responsible for a number of fatal attacks upon bathers in the West Indies, East Africa, Australia and elsewhere. It was common enough in the Gulf of Aden, where one night thirteen were caught on a set-line, the largest being 12 feet 6 inches long. The jaws of this one, when removed, could easily be passed over the head and shoulders of a fisherman, with room to spare. However, those specimens had been eating masses of crabs and fish, a few odds and ends, and our bait – but no humans.

They were common at Singapore, too, attracted by the refuse in the harbour. Young boys used to dive down to pick up coins thrown from the ships by tourists and on one occasion a lad was bitten in two by what was probably a Tiger Shark. But, as so often happens, I have to write 'probably', for unless a tooth were left behind there was no way of being sure. That was the only case I recall in a sojourn of about eight years in the area.

This species, being largely a bottom feeder, takes a good many things such as crabs and very often sting rays, the poison spines of which seem not to worry it. It is also a great robber of fishermen, taking bait and fish from hooks, biting lumps out of other sharks that have been caught, or tearing nets apart to get at the fish inside. Yet it can be of

Above left The Black-tipped Shark, one of the less dangerous of the cub sharks, shows the characteristic features of the selachians – large nostrils with flaps, inferior mouth, five external gill openings, and the form of the tail.

Above The White-tipped Shark, despite its rather ferocious aspect, is a sluggish creature which has not been definitely implicated in attacks on man.

commercial value for its skin, which makes good leather, and for the oil in its liver. The latter, however, is very variable, depending on the condition of the shark and whether or not it is breeding. A female with young often has little oil. We found from fifteen to thirty-eight young in the broods, little fellows a foot long, but they are often more numerous than that and in one case at Cuba as many as eighty-two were recorded.

No Tiger Shark has been observed in British waters or even in the Mediterranean, but it occurs off Morocco and the Canary Isles and down the African coast. It is common on the American coasts, especially the Carolinas and Florida, in the Caribbean and southward to Brazil and Uruguay. As already made clear, it is also plentiful in the Indian Ocean and through the East Indies to Australia and the Pacific. Enthusiasts should therefore have ample opportunity to make its acquaintance.

One shark that has an evil reputation is *Carcharhinus gangeticus* or, as some would have it, *C. leucas*. There is some dispute as to whether the Ganges Shark is different from the species that infests river-mouths in the rest of the tropics. It is claimed that it has two extra small teeth on each side. *C. gangeticus* travels well up the rivers around the Bay of Bengal and accounts for a number of deaths each year. Similarly, *C. leucas* can pass into freshwater and has been credited with a number of fatalities around Africa, the Americas and the western Pacific. It was a *C. leucas* that bit off the arm of Miss K. H. Passaris while she was swimming in only 5 feet of water at Broome in Australia. She fortunately recovered. An interesting thing is that the shark was caught with the undigested arm still in its stomach five days later. This delay in

Above The Grey Reef Shark, *Carcharhinus menisorrah,* is very common throughout the Indo-Pacific region and sometimes grows large enough to be dangerous to swimmers. This specimen is a male as shown by the large claspers on the pelvic fins.

digestion has been noted in other cases and the reason is not at present understood; the digestive process in sharks is otherwise rather rapid.

Carcharhinid sharks are often very numerous. It has been reckoned that the White-tipped Shark, *Carcharhinus longimanus*, may be the most abundant large animal (that is, weighing over 100 pounds) in existence. Fortunately, this is a rather sluggish species that has not definitely been proved to attack man, though it is suspected. It grows to a length of 15 feet so its bite could be very serious. It is at once recognizable by the very large pectoral fins, the lobes of which, like the dorsal fin, are broadly rounded, and by the snowy white tips of these fins, which are visible at a considerable distance. When tuna are feeding on schools of smaller fishes the White-tips have been seen to form a sort of fence around the mass and hold their jaws open so that tuna in their frenzied leaping will literally fall into their mouths. It will be seen therefore that, although apparently lazy, they are cunning and resourceful and not to be trusted too far.

For sheer numbers I would say that the Blue Shark, *Prionace glauca*, rivals the White-tip, for it is seen in large processions in the open ocean at certain times of the year, probably on migration. It is found on British coasts in summer, especially off Cornwall where thousands are caught by anglers. It is a very beautiful creature, slender and stream-lined – length for length it is much less heavy than others of the group – as befits a fast, ocean-going animal and is splendidly blue on the upper parts with white below. My own acquaintance with the Blue Shark has been from the decks of trawlers, for the blood, guts and trash washed out through the scuppers after a haul will encourage this species to follow the ship by day and night. One six-footer actually went into the trawl as it was being hauled. It was put in the ice-hold for the Museum, where it was eventually cast in plaster and then preserved for study.

It is fortunate that this shark, beautiful as it is, does not venture into shallow water on our own coasts, for it would do much to diminish the popularity of Torquay or Falmouth. In Australia, where it is known as the Blue Whaler, it has been responsible for a number of attacks. The snout of this shark is long; to bite it must either override the prey or come against it at an angle. In the old days when whales were cut up

The Whaler's slender, streamlined body is suited to its ocean-going mode of life.

alongside the ship Blue Sharks would help themselves to the meat and the angry crews found it practically impossible to drive them off, hence the name 'Whaler'. The fact that they were attracted and so difficult to discourage marks them as likely candidates for the role of man-slayer.

Sharks first locate their food either by hearing a commotion or by smell – sometimes by both. A wounded fish will struggle and its blood will taint the water; a shark may detect both from a distance of 200 yards or more. When the prey is within sight – at perhaps 15 yards – the shark will circle round, viewing it with one eye and reducing the radius of the circle to bring it closer. As the shark moves forward to seize the prey it is blind, for with the eyes at the side it cannot see straight ahead; but at this point sensory organs on the snout and the front of the head take over, informing the shark of what is happening immediately in front of it. For this reason the animal will often bring the snout tip right up to its quarry and knock it sharply to test its size, weight and degree of activity. The shoving behaviour mentioned earlier is not quite the same, though it may be an extension of the same movement.

The importance of the sense of smell may have something to do with the extraordinary shape of the head in the hammerhead sharks. In these, the sides of the skull are stretched out sideways so that the eyes are far apart on long flat blades. Without this distortion these sharks would be scarcely distinguishable from carcharhinids. An interesting thing is that there is almost a series from the carcharhinid shape to the most extreme development. First there is the Bonnet Shark, *Sphyrna tiburo*, with a somewhat broad head, then several species with the side blades getting wider, the result of this being that the inner groove of the nostril gets longer and longer. Then there is a further development, where the *outer* groove becomes lengthened as well, pushing the eyes still further apart; this is the most extreme and weird-looking head of *Sphyrna blochi*. The 'hammer' has puzzled zoologists for a long time; some have supposed it to be 'epibatic' (giving a lift to the head) but carcharhinids get along without it.

The several variations of the theme show that this is a comparatively recent development, still in the experimental stage. It seems to me evident that in these sharks the sense of smell is being improved at the expense of sight, the eyes being less effective the wider apart they are. But a study of these animals in their natural environment might reveal some advantage in the 'hammer' so far unsuspected.

Hammerheads are voracious and potentially dangerous, but most of them are comparatively small. The Great Hammerhead (*Sphyrna mokarran*), however, can be a killer. It grows to 15 feet or more, not becoming mature till it is 10 feet long. Whether guided by smell or any other sense it comes straight at anything it recognizes as food when it is hungry. The fact that it rarely circles round suggests again that its eyesight is not so good as that of carcharhinids. Fortunately it does not often come close inshore (though I have seen a small one caught in a beach seine) but is most often to be found on the outer side of a reef, near deepening water. The venturesome skin diver is therefore the most likely to meet this one. Fortunately again, this shark does not usually come with a rush but follows its nose warily and is so immediately recognizable that a good swimmer has a chance to take evasive action.

The scientific name *mokarran* is actually the Arabic name given to this species in the Red Sea and the adjacent parts of the Indian ocean where it is particularly common. But it has a world-wide tropical distribution.

As usual, Australia has the most trouble, either with this species or with *Sphyrna lewini*, which may enter estuaries. There seems to be something about Australia that brings out the worst in marine animals. Hammerheads have been responsible for a number of deaths there. Cases are also reported in the Atlantic, on Central American coasts and at least one at Florida (though the species was not determined). It is not certain that all cases refer to *Sphyrna mokarran*, for it takes an expert to distinguish one hammerhead from another. On the American coast the culprit may be *S. zygaena* which grows almost as large (up to 12 feet long) and comes inshore – even occasionally into freshwater. That species often moves up the American coast in summer in considerable numbers, reaching as far as New York, but they are mainly small ones probably born not long before, in course of dispersal.

The eggs in all sharks are fertilized internally. The male has a pair of 'claspers' which are modified parts of the pelvic fins. When pairing he inserts one of these into the genital opening of the female, where it may anchor by means of rough spines or hooks. Not uncommonly the male seizes a fin of the female with his mouth, not biting but often leaving light scratches on the skin. There is, however, a good deal of variety in the behaviour, to judge by the shape and structure of the claspers found in different species. Unfortunately most of our knowledge about this is by inference, since it is unusual to see sharks *in copula*. Smaller species kept in aquaria have been seen to pair; in the Spotted Dogfish the male wraps himself round the female to bring a clasper into position. Larger and less slender sharks cannot do this and must lie side by side, which is why only one clasper is used at a time. Female sharks have two ovaries and two oviducts, so it seems to me likely that the male changes sides, using the other clasper.

When sharks swim in company they are usually of a size and take care to keep away from groups of larger sharks. This segregation might happen because those of different sizes cruise at different speeds, but it is more likely that it results from the smaller ones' fear of the larger. In many species sharks are aggressive to those smaller than themselves and even cannibalistic. Not many animals eat selachians; the main threat comes from larger sharks.

In the ovoviviparous species (when the eggs hatch within the female and the young remain there until ready to fend for themselves) the embryos that enter the oviduct first often eat those that lag behind. Biologically this is advantageous since it eliminates the weak specimens and makes their space and nutriment available to the stronger ones, thereby increasing their chance of survival when they are released into the hurly-burly of the ocean.

It is hardly surprising to find that the groups of sharks which have the worst reputation for aggressive behaviour begin their lives in this way. The lamnids do, for example. The Porbeagle, *Lamna nasus*, is a common visitor to inshore waters in summer. The name *Lamna* was probably originally intended to be *Lamia*, a Greek name used for a shark and also applied to a mythic, cannibalistic female with whom mothers in ancient Greece used to scare their children into obedience. Certainly this shark is cannibalistic when young, for it is rare to find more than one foetus in each oviduct. The free-swimming animal feeds mainly on fish but has on rare occasions been known to try humans for a change. Its relative the Mackerel Shark, *Isurus oxyrinchus*, is also found off British shores but has not so far claimed a human victim to my

The Wobbegong of Australian
waters is also known as the
'Carpet Shark' owing to its
fringed edges.

knowledge, though on the American side of the Atlantic it is believed to have been the attacker in several cases. In the Pacific it is represented by the closely related Mako, *Isurus glaucus*, which originally achieved fame as a sporting fish in New Zealand. The name Mako is a Maori word and is now extended by anglers to cover the Atlantic species also.

All these are rather stream-lined species, with one or more keels on each side of the tail (a device found in many fishes to reduce drag caused by eddies and therefore indicating a swift swimmer). The head is not flattened as in the carcharhinids and the jaws can be protruded forward somewhat to grasp the prey with the dagger-like front teeth. The Porbeagle is a fairly stout species, no doubt capable of catching fish but prone also to taking those already caught on long-lines, to the annoyance of fishermen. It may sometimes be seen sunning itself with the dorsal fin above water – not by any means an exuberant animal.

The Makos, on the other hand, are agile and swift, famous for their habit of leaping high from the water. It is not always certain why these leaps are made, but in some cases it is part of a battle that is being fought with a swordfish or marlin. Although consuming a great quantity of ordinary fish such as mackerel, the Makos will also pursue much larger prey, particularly the Broadbill Swordfish, *Xiphias gladius*, and occasionally marlins and sailfish. The 'swords' of these fishes are formidable weapons that have often been driven through ships' timbers and it is understandable that if a swordfish charges with the great speed of which it is capable, the Mako's safest bet is to shoot out of the water and let it pass underneath. This leaping reflex to avoid unpleasantness operates also when the shark is hooked, making it a spectacular quarry for the angler.

It is obvious that a shark normally including large animals in its diet is more likely than others to take a human in its stride and it is fortunate that Makos are, on the whole, ocean-going creatures seldom entering harbours or river mouths where swimmers might come within their reach.

Unfortunately this is not true of the remaining, and by far the largest, member of this family, the notorious White Shark, *Carcharodon carcharias*. This has been so demonstrably involved in so many incidents resulting in the mutilation or death of humans that it is often referred to as the Man-eater. It does not, of course, really prowl the seas searching for a man to eat. Its normal diet consists of fish and squids, but as it usually grows to around 20 feet in length and has been known to reach 36 feet, it includes a number of larger animals as they become available, such as seals, turtles and other sharks. It is necessary to repeat that man is not a part of the marine fauna and if he insists in intruding himself into an alien medium he does so at his own risk. Even so, the selachian is not expecting to meet him and at least one White Shark turned and fled at the sight of a human. But that was the formidable Captain Cousteau.

According to Rondelet, writing in the sixteenth century, *Carcharodon* grew to a huge size in the vicinity of Nice and Marseilles and whole men in armour were found inside them. It is curious that among later records it is difficult to find one instance where a whole human body was found in a shark, whereas in Rondelet's time they appear to have been commonplace. One may only suppose that the Mediterranean at that time was a great dumping-ground for corpses, for it is not certain that these warriors were alive when eaten – indeed in one case the body was headless. It cannot be denied, however, that the White Shark grows large enough to swallow a human being entire: whole seals, large tuna, sharks of 6 feet or so in length, and, in one case, a whole horse have been found in captured specimens. The White Shark, like any other, is not above taking food already laid out for it; it will often take fish from set-lines and some specimens have been caught with an assortment of hooks and snoods inside them.

While the front teeth of the Makos and the Porbeagle are longer and more dagger-like than those behind, those of the White Shark are not. The arrangement reminds us more of that in the cub shark – an evenly graduated row in each jaw, those in the lower jaw slender for grasping, those in the upper broader and flatter for shearing. In large specimens the exposed part of an upper tooth appears as an equilateral triangle. The whole apparatus is made more efficient by having strong saw-like edges to every tooth; little side to side movement is required to take a clean bite.

In past ages there have been other species of *Carcharodon*, some of them several times larger than *C. carcharias* to judge from their teeth which have been dredged up from the ocean floor, but only the one species appears to have survived to the present time. It is found in all warm seas and sometimes, in summer, as far north as Newfoundland and Nova Scotia. It may occur on British coasts, though there has been no attack on a human to date. On South African coasts, where it has been involved in a number of incidents, it is known as the White Pointer. It is most common in the Australian region, where shark nets are needed to protect popular beaches, but it is seldom possible to identify the species concerned and it would seem that *Carcharodon* is often blamed for damage wrought by the large 'whalers'.

The White Shark is nowhere found in abundance, fortunately. It seems not to be gregarious but turns up, one here, one there, at widely separated places. It is essentially ocean-going but can be found in sur-prisingly shallow water – attacks have even occurred on people wading in the surf. It very commonly attacks small boats and will sometimes leave its card, for the teeth are rather brittle and pieces remain imbedded in the hull; in one or two cases fragments of teeth have been left in the flesh of its victims as a rare proof of identity.

The White Shark is not entirely white; its colour varies from bluish-grey through ash-grey to brown above, and the underside is pale grey to white. It has a single keel on each side of the tail, and the lobes of the caudal fin – like those of its brethren the Makos – are more nearly alike than in most sharks. Very little is known about its breeding habits except that it is ovoviviparous. The largest number of young recorded from a female was nine, each around 10 pounds in weight and about 2 feet in length. Usually there are fewer for as already mentioned they tend to be cannibalistic.

Only one other group of sharks is sufficiently dangerous to be in-cluded here – the sand sharks of the genus *Carcharias*. They have great bristly front teeth like those of the lamnids but are much more sluggish, sometimes lying around in groups in sandy bays. The pre-hensile teeth are excellent grabs for lifting various invertebrates from the sand and for grasping slower-moving fish. The common American species, *Carcharias taurus*, is considered harmless and holiday makers sometimes play with it, but in the Indo-Pacific region there are two or three species that are feared, particularly *Carcharias tricuspidatus* of India

Following pages During the making of a film, a Great White Shark repeatedly attacked the cage in which the camera man was working.

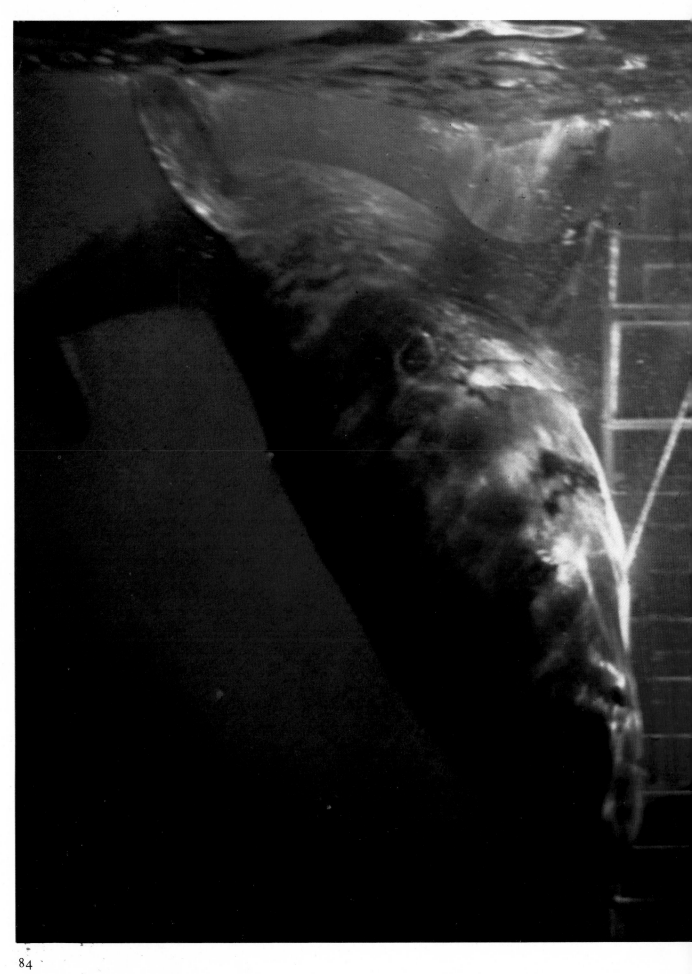

and the Malayan region and *Carcharias arenarius* of Australia. They may grow to 11 or 12 feet long and can inflict frightful wounds on the incautious swimmer. A large specimen which was among our haul on the Somali coast dragged itself about the deck lunging with spiked jaws at any legs it could reach; the crew were kept well exercised until it could be quietened.

One of the most frightening things about sharks is their tenacity of life. Long after they appear to be dead they may snap with the jaws or lash with the tail. There are records of sharks swimming around in the sea after their jaws have been cut out as trophies, or actually trying to feed after internal organs have been removed. It is difficult not to feel sorrow at such ruin of creatures that were so splendid and terrible in their prime.

Sharks are alarming things, but even in tropical areas the chance of being involved in an incident is very small. In a place where there have been cases in the past, do not go swimming or diving alone. Wear as much clothing as possible, preferably a dark colour – bare skin and light clothing attract sharks. Do not spear fish and particularly do not spear or otherwise molest sharks. If one of them comes close in a menacing manner hit it on the nose with something hard – if you use your hand the rough skin may damage it. Never fool about with any shark as an act of bravado, for even the 'harmless' ones can inflict injury if annoyed. On the other hand do not panic. If a shark comes into view make no sudden commotion but swim away smoothly and rhythmically and leave the water as soon as possible. Keep out of the sea at night, for that is the time many sharks feed.

If in spite of all this an injury should occur, it is a surgical job and the only thing to do is to try to prevent loss of blood. Get the victim out of the water as soon as possible and call medical aid immediately.

Sharks often have a small fold or groove at each corner of the mouth, which gives them the appearance of smiling gently as they move forward to show you that they like you so much they could eat you. Crocodiles, as Lewis Carroll noted long ago, have that same smile. There actually is a crocodile that swims in the sea (no doubt related to the one with Captain Hook's clock in it). What is more, it is the largest species known – the Estuarine Crocodile, *Crocodylus porosus*. There was a time when it was very common in all the rivers and estuaries of the Indo-Australian region and was reported to reach 40 feet in length.

However, because it is considered an undesirable neighbour by the village communities and even more because its skin is a valuable article of commerce, it is now getting rare and is seldom allowed to reach any impressive size. Indeed, it has to be 'farmed' in order to meet the demand for skins, but this 'farming' is itself threatening the survival of the species in Malaya. The crocodiles are not being bred, as one might suppose; all that happens is that eggs or newly hatched young are collected in the wild and brought to the 'farms' to be grown to a commercial size. These farms are usually run as an adjunct to pig farms, so that unwanted young or parts of pigs can be used as food for the crocodiles. When the latter reach the necessary girth they are killed and skinned.

At one of these farms I saw one of the assistants seized by the arm by a 4 foot long crocodile. It took several minutes to force it to release its hold, leaving a series of nasty holes. On another occasion, in a pet shop in London, the same thing happened to a lady assistant, that time

The Killer Whale has a distinctive, high dorsal fin.

Upper This sand shark, *Carcharias arenarius,* is known as the Grey Nurse in Australia where it has been responsible for a number of attacks on swimmers.

Lower A baby White-tipped Shark is shown at the moment of birth.

Right A Killer Whale performing at the Miami Seaquarium.

with a young Gharial – a slender-snouted crocodile – that she was showing to a customer. A key had to be inserted and twisted to force its jaws apart and release her. Once a crocodile clamps its jaws on something it seems to have difficulty in relaxing them.

The teeth of a crocodile are peg-like and used for gripping: they cannot cut or chew. If, therefore, it seizes something too large to be swallowed it twists and rolls until a manageable piece is wrenched off. However, a large estuarine crocodile could take most ordinary animals in one piece. The largest specimen actually recorded scientifically was 33 feet long with a girth round the middle of 13 feet 8 inches; it could easily have consumed a human being at a gulp.

The normal habitat of this reptile is the estuaries of large rivers and the muddy swamps and pools that lie near them, though small ones are often found well upstream in fresh water. To move from one estuary to another they must, of course, go out to sea and it is only then that they come within the compass of this book.

Formerly they were common along the Queensland coast of Australia but here again they have been reduced in numbers to such an extent that they are no longer a serious hazard to swimmers. They are, however, of great zoological interest and it would be sad if they became extinct. They are the survivors of an ancient race related to the dinosaurs and thus, surprisingly, the nearest living relatives of the birds.

Yet one more smiling predator needs to be mentioned – the Killer Whale, *Orcinus orca*.

When a small boy I saw the film taken by Ponting on the ill-fated Scott expedition to the Antarctic. One shot that left a lasting impression on my mind was of enormous black and white bodies hurling themselves out of the water and slithering across the ice, trying to seize the dogs of the sledge teams. The Killer Whale was from that time established for me as one of the most frightful things to be found in the sea. This view was further strengthened by the old textbooks which informed me that the Killer grew to a length of 20 feet; that it could devour four ordinary porpoises in a row; that a specimen rather less than 16 feet long had fourteen seals in its stomach; that it was commonly observed to hunt in packs and attack the larger whales, devouring them. Clearly a man would be but a mouthful to such a monster. Yet it is now being kept as a pet in more than one oceanarium, where it performs tricks and lets its keeper put his head in its mouth.

The Killer Whale is really only a very large kind of dolphin and can be as entertaining as its smaller brethren. The face of any dolphin wears a smile and the killer can appear quite jovial. The male has a high dorsal fin that grows very tall with age and bends over at the tip, so that at a certain angle it looks like a long neck with a small head on it when seen above the surface of the water. I think indistinct photographs of this may have been passed off as snaps of sea serpents or loch monsters.

Killers are found in all seas, mostly in open water but sometimes entering estuaries. They have even been up the River Thames in former times. But unless I go swimming among a bevy of seals or porpoises I shall no longer fear ending my days as a second Jonah.

Aggressive fish

Besides sharks there are several kinds of true fish that have been accused of aggression against man, though it is even less likely in most cases that they are trying to eat him. Looking at the various reports it would seem that the instances of aggression can be placed in one or other of the following categories: defence of territory, fear reaction, accident, very rarely predation.

Groupers, perch-like fish of the genus *Serranus* and its relatives, often mark out territories for themselves. The young are very common in tide pools but as they grow each one finds a cranny for itself in deeper water and stays there for a long period. If it grows very large in the course of years it goes deeper still. Completely submerged old wrecks well offshore sometimes harbour one or two giants. Or at least I hope some of them still do: the invention of the aqualung and the spear gun has resulted in wholesale and useless slaughter of groupers, for they will rush out fearlessly to defend the home in which they have spent a large part of their lives. When one of them is killed it is a long time before another takes its place – possibly never at the present merciless rate of the 'sport'. One species, the Giant Bass, *Promicrops lanceolatus*, grows to a length of 8 feet or more and a girth of maybe 5 feet, for it is a great, barrel-like fellow. This is the sort that can make a wrecked ship its home. It has very small teeth but a huge mouth and it could easily swallow a man simply by sucking him in. It could also accommodate a spear gun or two in its belly and is the last hope of its tribe against the tide of destruction.

As any experienced skin diver knows, outright aggression is common behaviour with certain moray eels. It is usually called 'unprovoked aggression' but from the moray's point of view it is provoking to have a hulking great creature casting a shadow over its lair or otherwise upsetting the familiar prospect. On the other hand, the moray is usually lying with head peeping out, ready to take a bite at anything luscious that happens to pass by: it is not just lying there, but lurking. So a bite from a moray may fall into one or both of two of our categories – defence of territory or predation. Certainly it is difficult to accuse it of

Left The Giant Bass, *Promicrops lanceolatus,* grows large enough to swallow a man, but such monsters are not likely to be found close to the shore. When very young this species is prettily marked with yellow and black.

Above A moray eel showing the knife-like teeth on the roof of the mouth. The fierce aspect of this specimen does not belie its nature: morays are often aggressive when disturbed.

fear – rather the reverse, for it will chase a man out of the water and up the beach.

Morays are true eels – they have no pelvic fins and the dorsal and anal fins meet round the end of the tail. A number of families with these characteristics are grouped together in the order Apodes ('footless') though there are considerable differences in the skulls and it is very likely that they were not originally related but have come to look alike by losing so many bits and pieces. If the tail fin of any fish is lost, in early life for instance, the dorsal and anal fins will grow round to fill its place. This may have happened to the eels genetically and happened more than once. However, this is not a subject to pursue here.

The morays have no obvious gill covers but possess a gill opening behind the eye on each side. They have a formidable array of dagger-like teeth. There are no scales, no pectoral fins and the dorsal and anal

Above A large Giant Bass.

Below It is possible that the large mackerel known as the Wahoo or Peto (*Acanthocybium solandri*) is

94

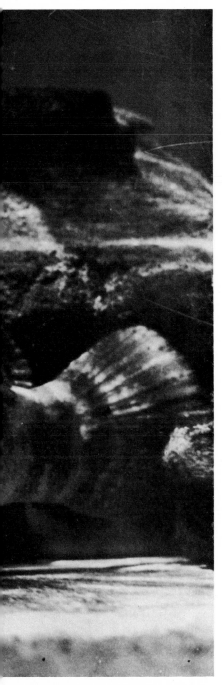

fins are often just folds of thick skin. Some of the species are quite brightly coloured but nearly always variegated to blend with the coral or rock surround.

The common Mediterranean species, *Muraena helena*, was kept in stock ponds as food and, if ancient writers are to be believed, fed on the bodies of slaves to improve their flavour. There are several other genera and most of those met in the tropics belong to the genus *Gymnothorax*. In some places one may find a member of some species in practically every crevice or hole along a rocky shore; not much else has a chance to take possession of such desirable residences in the face of these aggressive animals. Most of them are only two or three feet long – the really big ones are more often found further out on the reefs, where they lie entwined in the coral, heads protruding with mouths agape. One of 7 feet in length is a big one, though they often seem larger because of their strength, agility and ferocity.

The largest eel I ever saw belonged to a quite different family with pectoral fins. It was a specimen of *Muraenesox cinereus*, 11 feet long, give or take an inch or two. The name *Muraenesox* means pike-moray and it is appropriate, for this beast has long, pointed jaws with a jagged assortment of teeth, not unlike the mouth of a pike. It is lucky that this fish prefers deeper water.

Perhaps the worst reputation next to that of the sharks is held by the barracuda, which has been alleged to attack at sight and bite pieces out of people. This behaviour is credited to the genus *Sphyraena*, of which there are several species. At first sight they somewhat resemble the common freshwater Pike, though they are not related. Barracudas have spiny fins that show their affinities with the perch-like fishes.

Until I made their acquaintance at first hand I used to put these fishes down as killers, following the accounts given by numerous writers before me, but now I am not so sure. It appears to me that in some cases the *Sphyraena* has been the victim of mistaken identity. My doubts were first aroused when I went down through a school of them. They were standing still in mid-water in the shelter of a large cave. As I went down a few of them moved gracefully aside to let me through and when I came up with a netful of odds and ends they did the same again. I was so much more interested in this than in my catch that a triggerfish bit a piece out of my thumb, making me almost faint with the pain. The teeth of the triggerfish can bore a neat hole in an oyster shell. However, to get back to the barracuda.

This was not the only time by any means that I hobnobbed with *Sphyraena* and I have spoken to other people who have had the same experience. So what is all this about ferocious attacks? A possible answer was suggested to me when I learned that the name barracuda is given to another fish. It is a Spanish name, I believe. Now, quite a long while ago a number of the larger species of the mackerel family known as tuna and bonito (also Spanish names) were found to be plentiful along the Californian and Mexican coasts, so a considerable fishery developed there, centred on San Diego. In the course of these operations, which often required the fishermen to stand knee-deep in water on racks slung over the side of the vessel, sharks were a constant nuisance and occasionally barracuda too. But *this* barracuda was a huge member of the mackerel group, with long savage jaws that could take off a hand quite easily. Whereas *Sphyraena* when caught will lie and die like any ordinary fish, the other barracuda, *Acanthocybium*, will fight

largely responsible for the attacks credited to the Barracuda. It is very swift and aggressive and could easily be mistaken for *Sphyraena*.

Barracuda *(Sphyraena)* often
swim lazily in large shoals.
Swimmers who encounter these
are rarely if ever attacked
despite the bad reputation of
these fish.

back and is as difficult to get under control as a wild cat. A San Diego fisherman assured me that it is feared more than the sharks. This is the fish known to anglers by its Hawaiian name Wahoo. Anglers regret and tuna fishermen rejoice that it is not very commonly encountered. It seems to me therefore that the reputation of the *Acanthocybium* barracuda has been to some extent grafted on to the *Sphyraena* barracuda by writers who supposed the name to apply to one fish. Which shows the importance of scientific names.

That being said, it has to be admitted that the Great Barracuda, *Sphyraena sphyraena*, grows to 6 feet or so in length and that the very large, knife-like teeth in its jaws look the kind of thing a man-eater should possess. It could give a bad bite if it felt inclined. But I do not think man is the sort of animal it usually attacks. De Sylva, writing in 1963, had searched the records back to 1873, that is for 90 years, finding only twenty-nine attacks (not all certainly identified) on swimmers. He says: 'The barracuda attacks only once, not repeatedly as do sharks. The wound is narrow, with two almost parallel rows of toothmarks, unlike that made by a shark, which is crescentic and jagged.'

This seems to me to exonerate *Sphyraena* because its really large teeth

The Barracuda, like the moray eels, carries its largest teeth on the roof of its mouth.

are on the palatine bones, in the middle of the upper jaw and the rows of smaller teeth along the edges of the jaws converge towards the tip. So *Sphyraena* could not make two almost parallel rows of marks; but the beak-like jaws of *Acanthocybium* could.

If my guess is correct, fishermen catching *Acanthocybium* on tuna poles are more likely to be bitten than swimmers. But I hope no one will aggravate a six-foot *Sphyraena* just to prove me wrong.

Some way back, when discussing the Mako, mention was made of the swordfish which sometimes do battle with it. For as long as

A number of cases are known of swimmers being pierced through by the long upper jaws of swordfish. Here a Broadbill Swordfish appears to be thrusting at the diver who has placed it in an oceanarium.

records go back there are accounts of attacks on boats by these fish and in museums there are pieces of ships' timbers pierced by the swords as proof.

The 'swords' or rostrums of these fish are great prolongations of the bones of the upper jaw. That in the Broadbill Swordfish, *Xiphias gladius*, is flattened, very likely in order to supply the 'lift' at the front end of the body that in other fishes would be provided by the pelvic fins (in the swordfish these have been lost). Basically, however, it is an extreme form of streamlining, as these are very swift fishes. The rostrums of the other families – the marlins or spearfish (Makairidae) and the sailfish (Istiophoridae) – are narrower and round in section. All these animals grow large – 6 feet long or more – so their principal enemies are larger still, the swift sharks and certain of the dolphins. It is thus hardly surprising that they should lunge at a boat that looks like a great predator cruising overhead. So far I have not found any account which suggested that any one of these fish deliberately stalked a boat or man: it seems always to be a fear reaction or an accident.

These fish are among the fastest known – specimens have been clocked at 60 miles an hour. Even with the extreme shape, the power needed to drive more than 100 pounds of fish through the water at that speed is very great and the 'brakes' of these fish, as represented by the pectoral fins, are not very large, so they need a fair distance to pull up if something unexpected obstructs the way. As in so many other fish the eyes are at the sides of the head and cannot be focused on anything a short distance ahead, so with visibility at perhaps 15 to 20 feet the spearfish travelling at 60 miles an hour will never see the object.

If the unexpected object happens to be a human being the result is likely to be fatal to the person concerned. Norman mentions a record of a man being killed by a 'swordfish' in the river Severn, quoting Daniel's 'Rural Sports'. That was probably a sailfish, as in my time (somewhat later than Daniel's) a specimen of *Istiophorus americanus* was taken in that same river. In old records the distinction between swordfish, marlin and sailfish was not made. The sailfish gets its name from the very large expanse of the first dorsal fin; it is generally lighter than the marlins and does not grow so large.

Odd cases of men being impaled, always accidentally I think, occur from time to time. A man died in 1960 after being pierced through the abdomen. Another case occurred in 1965 somewhere in Polynesia (although reported upon by four doctors they neglected to mention where it happened). The fish was identified as an 'Espadon à voile' (Sailfish) *Istiophorus gladius*, which drove its spear right through the thorax of a young fisherman, from chest to vertebral column, making a hole 'about the size of a five-franc piece'. It passed through the diaphragm, through the left lobe of the liver and through the diaphragm again before hitting a vertebra, but the doctors, whatever their documentary inadequacies, sewed him together in the right places, gave him the right antibiotics and he recovered.

This kind of hazard is obviously rare in the sea, but if it happens there is nothing you can do about it except hope that four good doctors will do the right things. It is the least of the risks you take when you pass out of your own element into another.

99

Poisonous and venomous fish

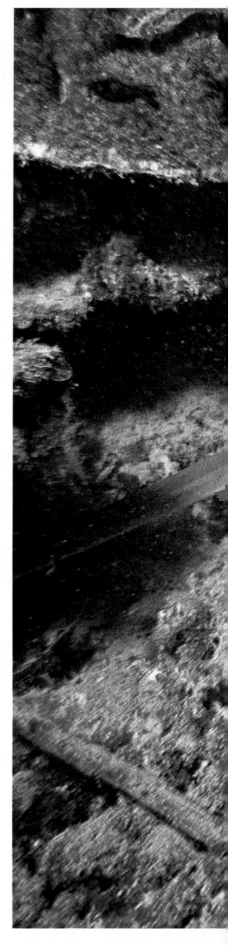

Some people are allergic to fish and break out into spots after eating it unless they take antihistamine pills. But there are numerous species of fish, especially in the tropics, that are poisonous to anybody if eaten at the wrong time and some that are poisonous to anybody at any time. This is mainly true of the pufferfish and their relatives, of which about seventy-five species are known to be toxic to man. These fish have a specific poison known as tetrodotoxin. It is present in most of their tissues but is particularly concentrated in the ovaries and liver. Captain Cook found this out the hard way in 1774. While his ship was at New Caledonia his artist took rather a long time to make a drawing of a new kind of puffer, so it was considered too stale to be cooked. Cook and his officers decided therefore to try a little of the liver – just about the worst part they could have picked upon. Needless to say, they were very ill that night, and a pig which was given the rest of the entrails was found dead next morning.

In the face of this it is rather surprising to find that some kinds of puffer are considered a delicacy in Japan – but only when prepared in special restaurants where the cooks have been trained and granted a government certificate.

In various parts of the East at least a hundred people die from tetrodotoxin poisoning each year – rather more than half the cases reported. A great deal of research has been done to discover the nature of the poison and it is now known to be a very potent non-protein of complicated structure. It is prepared commercially as TTX and is of some value in pharmacology.

It is disturbing to find that a large number of fish, many of them belonging to groups we consider our best food-fish, such as herrings and tuna, may at times have poisonous flesh. About eight hundred species have been found, at some time or another, to produce the ailment known as ciguatera. It seems fairly certain that the poison comes in the first place from algae upon which lower organisms have been feeding; then the fish eats the lower organisms and man eats the fish. In some cases it may be more direct: the algae may be those that live

in corals, so that fish feeding on coral are likely to get high concentrations in their flesh. A high proportion of ciguatera-producing fish come from coral reefs.

A substance isolated as ciguatoxin is found also in other groups such as molluscs, arthropods, echinoderms and even newts in freshwater. It is highly complex and may not be a single substance. Moreover, some of the symptoms of the disease may be caused by other substances that vary from one kind of animal to another according to the food-chain: it may even be that the dinoflagellates encountered earlier are involved somewhere. It is best to designate all these cases under the general name ichthyotoxism (fish poisoning) which causes great disturbance of the stomach and intestines, vomiting, diarrhoea, weakness of the legs and paralysis, and in the worst cases, cyanosis, collapse and asphyxiation.

Another sort of poisoning – the secreting of a toxic substance from the skin – is used by certain kinds of fish for defence. The slime of lampreys has long been claimed to be poisonous, which may possibly account for the reputed death of King John from a 'surfeit of lampreys'. (It was Henry I, in fact, who died of eating lampreys – John exacted 40 marks from the men of Gloucester because 'they did not pay him sufficient respect in the matter of lampreys'.) The attractive boxfish or trunkfish (Ostraciontidae) when alarmed secrete a poison from their skins which can kill other fish – a point to be noted by devotees of the tropical marine aquarium.

It is but a step from this to the development of a device to inject the poison into the body of whatever enemy gets too attentive. A great many fish have sharp spines supporting parts of their dorsal, anal and pelvic fins, which serve for defence merely by their ability to stab: the enemy can be stopped in his tracks long enough for the fish to dart away. But some species, mostly of a sluggish nature, combine these spines, or others on the gill covers, with venom-secreting glands or tissue, so that the enemy is not just pricked but is convulsed and disabled and there is no need for the sluggish character to do any darting away.

Fish that do this sort of thing are usually described as venomous, to distinguish them from those that are poisonous when eaten. About two hundred of them are known, mostly belonging to the mail-cheeked group that includes the weevers, scorpionfishes and stonefishes. It is unnecessary to mention all of them here, for many of them are very much alike. The results of their stings are alike, too, in one important respect – they all produce intense pain, indicating that their main function is deterrent. In the case of aggressive or predaceous animals such as snakes the need is simply to kill the victim, not to make it suffer, so their bite is not as agonizing.

It seems likely that the pain producing element in all the venomous fish is the same, though it is not the only ingredient of the toxin, which as usual is rather complicated. However much they may vary in composition, these toxins are quite unlike the toxins found in poisonous fish. Even a poisonous and a venomous fish from the same group have toxins of a quite different nature. The toxins of poisonous (non-edible) fish, insofar as they can be characterized at present, appear to be complex oils with a lipid base, whereas those of venomous fish are proteins.

Some selachians – the stingrays – are venomous. Rays may be described as flattened sharks, although it is quite likely that the ancestors of both rays and sharks were flattened and that the round-bodied, mid-water

Preceding pages One of the prettiest rays is the Blue-spotted Stingray, *Taeniura lymma*, of Indian and Pacific waters.

Right A stingray moving along the sea floor by undulating its large pectoral fins. The barb on the tail is enlarged in the inset to show its toothed edge.

Below Many stingrays have two spines on the tail. It may be that one of these is a 'spare', as these spines seem often to be easily lost.

Following pages A favourite among keepers of marine aquaria, the beautifully coloured Lionfish, *Pterois antennata*, must be handled carefully. It is not aggressive, however, and soon becomes tame.

sharks came later, which is why they have inherited the ventrally placed mouth and gills and the spiracles. The spiracles are apertures behind the eyes, which are large in rays and the more primitive sharks but become smaller and are eventually lost in the more highly evolved sharks. Their function is to take in water that can be passed over the gills and pushed out through the gill slits underneath, leaving the mouth free to concentrate on feeding activities.

Most rays have very large pectoral fins, often called wings, by which they swim gracefully for short distances. These broad fins give them an almost circular shape with the narrow tail trailing behind, except in the guitarfishes (*Rhinobatos*) and the sawfishes (*Pristis*) which are narrower and somewhat more shark-like. I mention these because they provide the best quality 'shark fins' of commerce, in great demand for the delicious shark fin soup. Some of the sharks do provide fins, of course, but are less valuable than these rays.

Sawfish grow to a considerable size and with the great rigid blade or rostrum on the snout, beset with strong teeth on each side, they might be thought dangerous. Yet I have found them harmless enough and have still to be convinced that they dash into schools of fish mutilating them by slashing about with the 'saw'. According to my observations they lie around like any other ray and when they move about in search of food they use the rostrum not as a saw but as a rake, turning up the sand rhythmically from side to side and picking up the molluscs and other invertebrates that are flushed out.

Some rays, such as the Skate which is used as food, lay eggs in horny sheaths, but the stingrays, with which we are concerned, are ovoviviparous. There are many kinds, ranging in size from a few inches to 7 feet across the 'wings'. Only one, *Dasyatis pastinaca*, is occasionally found on British coasts. In the Mediterranean and the tropics they are a menace to those who handle them.

The 'sting' is a long, movable spine on the slender tail; in the adult it can be anything from 2 to 6 inches long. As it is found to be composed of dentine coated with enamel it is evident that it is just an enlarged, modified denticle. In some species there may be two or even three of them. The spine is saw-edged on each side, the teeth of the saw pointing forward, and below this is a groove filled with tissue that secretes venom into the skin covering the spine.

It is quite evident that this apparatus, as in most venomous fish, is for the defence of an animal that has no great turn of speed. If it is interfered with the ray will swing its tail over its back, inflicting a lacerated wound on the enemy with the saw-like spine and at the same time introducing the venom from the skin into the wound. Result: great pain and swelling, causing the enemy to think twice before trying again.

Stingrays are very common in river mouths, sandy bays and lagoons, where they lie buried in the sand with only the eyes, spiracles and part of the tail above the surface. In some places unspoiled by man (and how few these are becoming!) the bed of the sea seems to be paved with them as they glide away in successive, radiating groups as one's shadow passes over them.

Fishermen who find stingrays in their nets usually take them by the tail and cut off the spine immediately, but this is not always as simple as it sounds and experienced men may get stung. Apart from the instant and excruciating pain, the venom has a direct effect on heart muscle, but fortunately this very rarely results in death. There have been cases where swimmers have inadvertently trodden upon stingrays with resulting damage, usually to the ankle, that left them crippled for some time. It is said that a large one can drive its spine right through a limb or even a plank of wood.

Surprisingly, other fish sometimes eat them and they form a large part of the diet of the White Shark, whose stomach is often full of the spines, some of which pierce the muscular wall.

Coming now to the true fishes, we find special glands developed for the venom. Fish have a bony skeleton, the main features of which resemble ours – a skull, vertebral column, shoulder bones and pelvic bones. The shoulder bones are rather more complex than ours and support the pectoral fins which serve a number of important purposes, varying from one fish to another. The pelvic bones are small and usually simple, carrying the pelvic fins which serve either for balancing or steering. All the fins are supported by rods of bone called rays which are most often jointed and flexible, branching out towards the edge of the fin. But often the rays supporting the front part of the dorsal fin, the anal fin and the first ray of each pelvic fin are stiff, sharply pointed spines, hinged at the base, that can be raised or lowered at will. About two thirds of the known species of fish have such spines, which make them prickly to handle at the best of times but over a hundred of them are known to be venomous as well.

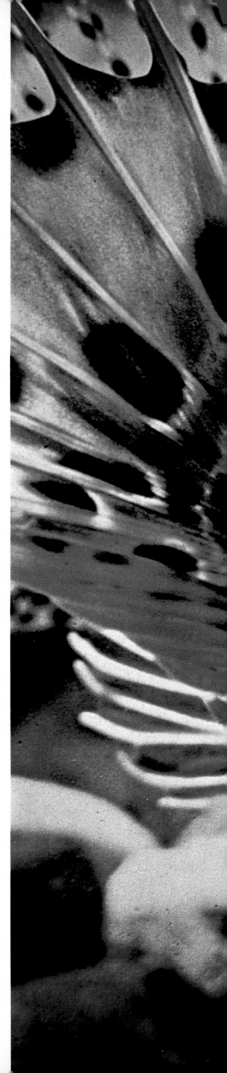

Catfish often have a single spine at the front of the dorsal fin and one on each pectoral fin, often with saw-like edges. Most of them are found in fresh water and some are popular aquarium fish, but one genus, *Plotosus*, that lives in the sea, is noted for its violent sting. This is a rather eel-like fish, with the dorsal and anal fins joining up with the tail fin, which moves in sinuous waves through the water, often in groups. It has, of course, the 'whiskers' that give catfish their name. When it is young it is very pretty with black and white bands along the sides and congregates in closely packed schools which are fascinating to watch. The whole mass of young fish swims with perfect coordination so that it appears to be a single individual weaving its way among the rocks and swerving aside at the approach of any disturbing element such as you or me. Even at that size, maybe 2 inches long, it is best to leave them alone. I had some in an aquarium once and in transporting them to another tank I caught a finger on one of the tiny spines – it was like being stung by an overgrown hornet and it pretty well doubled me up for a moment or two. Touching the sting with strong formalin eases the pain but of course this is poor advice unless you are in an institution or collecting for a museum.

The weeverfishes (the name comes from the Anglo-Saxon word

Looking very dangerous with its huge, toothed rostrum, the Sawfish is in fact harmless and uses the saw to turn molluscs and other food from the sand. It grows to a large size and provides high quality fins for soup.

wivere – viper), two species of which may be found on British coasts, have venomous spines not only on the dorsal fin but on the gill covers too. Indeed, those on the gill covers are more virulent than the others. There is a groove on the outer and inner sides of the spine, along which lies the translucent gland full of poison. The whole thing is covered by thin skin. Pressure on the tip of the spine causes it to break through the skin and the venom runs up the grooves into the punctured enemy. There are from five to eight less potent spines in the first dorsal fin, which is black and is left projecting above the sand as a warning; the equipment on the gill covers is apparently a second and more powerful line of defence.

According to Couch, a disturbed weever will strike deliberately with its head, aiming to this side or that with considerable accuracy. Of the two species the Lesser Weever is the more virulent and, as it inhabits areas where shrimp are abundant, it is likely to be included in the catch of shrimp fishermen, who must sort their catch warily. A hand stung by a weever swells to about twice its size and incapacitates the fisherman for some time.

Weever stings produce severe pain which reaches its peak in about thirty minutes, causing the victim to scream and lash about, even to

Stingrays are the more dangerous because they often lie buried in the sand with the eyes and the spiracles above the surface for seeing and breathing, and the poison spine exposed for the unwary to tread upon.

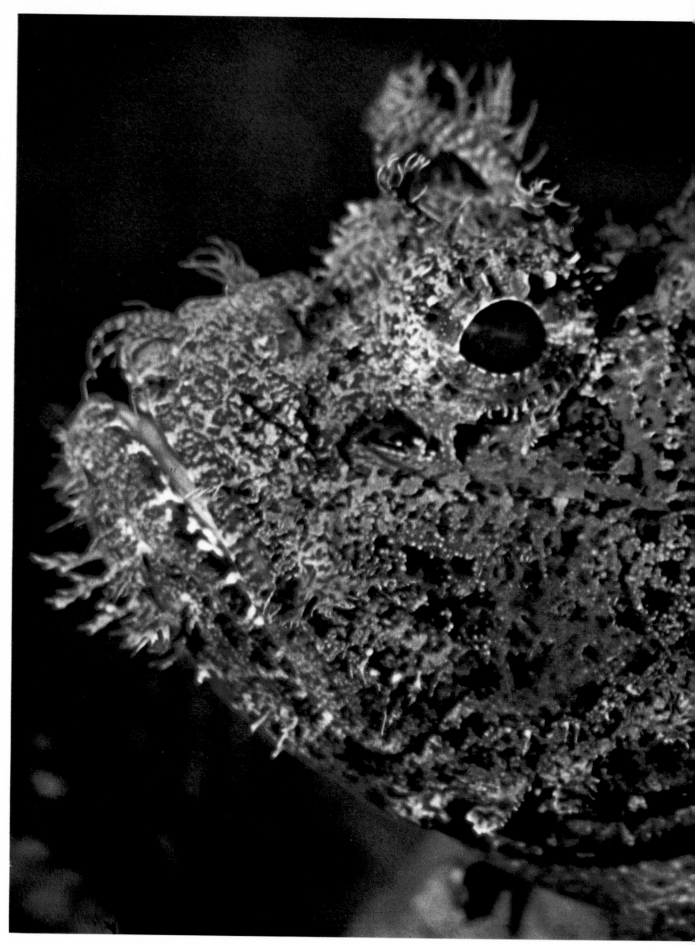

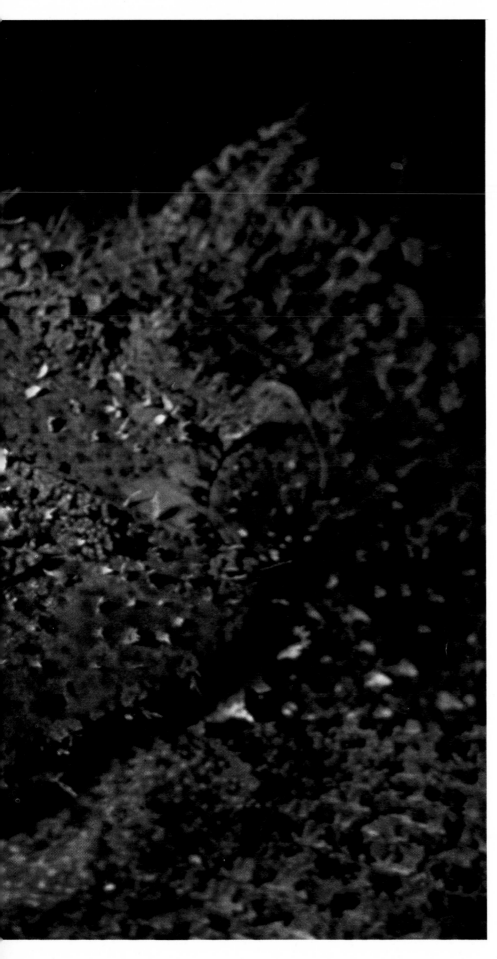

Scorpionfishes all have poison spines of greater or lesser potency and often show remarkable tricks of camouflage. This specimen would be difficult to spot among coralline growth.

lose consciousness. Delirium, dizziness, palpitation and vomiting are common and in severe cases there may be paralysis, convulsions, dyspnoea or heart-failure. Usually, however, the pain abates after twenty-four hours, giving place to numbness, but the skin remains red and swollen for up to ten days.

The Greater Weever, *Trachinus draco*, ranges from the Baltic to the Black Sea and is usually found in deep water: it is only likely to be troublesome to fishermen who must remove it from trawl or seine nets. But the Lesser Weever, *T. vipera*, which is common from the North Sea down to the Mediterranean, sometimes comes into shallow water and may be trodden upon by people wading with bare feet. This is the one responsible for most of the British fish stings.

It is advisable to wear rope-soled shoes when paddling or wading anywhere, not so much because of the remote possibility of being crippled by a weever as because of the much greater chance of treading on a broken bottle or jagged tin thrown there by animals of another kind.

In the Mediterranean and Atlantic there is a rather flat, inconspicuous fish with a very large mouth and strong fins on which it can walk about on the sea bed, called *Batrachoides didactylus*. It is one of the toadfishes (Batrachoididae) which have representatives in most parts of the world. A few of them, such as *Coryzichthys* are estuarine and can pass into fresh water; only recently some specimens were imported to Britain as novelties for the aquarium and aquarists will need to handle them carefully. They have a spine on the upper edge of each gill cover and two or three on the dorsal fin. The most dangerous genus is *Thalassophryne*. The spines of these fish are interesting in that they are hollow, so that the venom can be injected into a wound through the tip, after the manner of a snake's fangs.

All the scorpionfish have twelve to fifteen dorsal spines, three anal spines, and one spine on each pelvic fin. There is a great variety of these, found in the tropics and sub-tropics of the world. Two or three of the Mediterranean species occasionally find their way to the British

Many bathers have been stung by the Lesser Weever, *Trachinus vipera,* which may lie buried in sand with only the black poison spines (here lying flat) on the back protruding above the surface. The mouth and eyes look upwards to facilitate observation and attack.

coasts in summer, but so rarely that they are scarcely worth the mention.

In tropical waters, however, they are very numerous, inhabiting crannies in rocks, crevices in coral or lying partly buried in sand. They are often difficult to see as they are camouflaged with an elaborate pattern of patches and stripes and often have skinny flaps that make them look more like weed-covered rock than fish. Some of them are quite beautiful and tempting to touch. It is not possible to do justice to them here; there are some seven hundred species which, if each were described and illustrated, would make a couple of lovely volumes by themselves. One genus which has become fairly well known since the cult of the marine aquarium came into vogue is *Pterois*. No really suitable popular name has been found for this group – lionfish, dragonfish or turkeyfish give no hint of the rich pattern of stripes or the splendid radiate fins.

The one most commonly seen is *Pterois volitans*. This is a slow-moving fish, generally found near the surface and quite tame, for it has little need to fear anything. Several times I have tried to net one – it looked so easy – but without any apparent effort the fish contrived to be just outside the rim of the net each time. It reminded me of trying to creep up on a flock of flamingoes to photograph them. You walk and walk but the flock is always as far away as at the beginning, though there is no obvious movement. So with *Pterois*: it glides grandly through the water, calmly avoiding interference, with all fins spread like a spherical bunch of orange and black striped feathers. But the shaft of every 'feather' on the back has a sharp tip and can inject a virulent poison. There is, however, no need to be stung by this fish, for it is conspicuous enough to be avoided and only those handling it for the aquarium run any risk at all.

Not so the Stonefish, *Synanceja horrida*. This is as ugly as *Pterois* is beautiful. It is short, thick, lumpy and warty, with very small eyes set in large hollow sockets and the mouth set high. The colour is drab brown, with a flush of orange on the underside at breeding time. It grows only to about 9 inches long and closely resembles a lump of the stone among which it lives as it sits half buried in the sand waiting for something edible to come along.

The black poison spines of the Greater Weever, *Trachinus draco,* are well shown in this photograph and the even more virulent spines on the gill cover and shoulder are also visible.

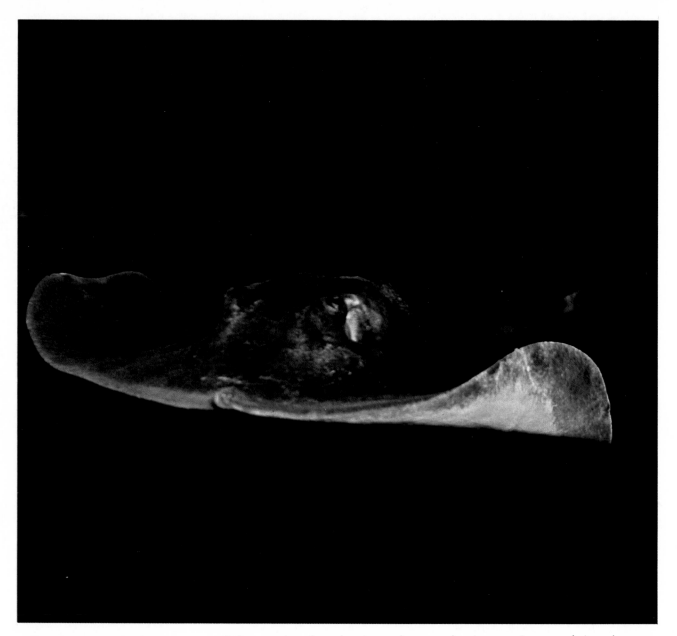

Above A stingray, *Dasyatis pastinaca,* glides through the water using its wing-like pectoral fins.

Opposite The beautiful *Pterois,* like a spherical bunch of orange and black striped feathers. The erect spines on the back are provided with poison glands and can inflict painful, though not serious, wounds.

It has twelve dorsal spines, three anal spines and two pelvic spines, all provided with venom glands. Unlike the others we have mentioned these glands are at the sides of the spines and very bulky, so that they contain a greater amount of toxin than any other fish. It has been estimated that one stonefish could kill as many as twenty-five thousand mice (though I don't believe so many would take up skin-diving). This compares with two thousand five hundred for *Pterois* and only one thousand for weevers.

I will not waste the next half page in describing the contortions and shrieks of those who step on a Stonefish barefooted. It has been stated that they will beg for the limb to be chopped off immediately or to be put out of their agony for good. They are, in fact, driven mad with pain. They may go into a coma. As with all such stings, a ligature should be placed above the wound (loosened at intervals to avoid gangrene). A hot compress with magnesium sulphate, or better still placing the whole foot in water as hot as the patient can bear, is recommended because heat breaks up the toxin. Treat the patient for shock and get him to hospital as soon as possible. A fall in blood pressure and

rapid breathing usually results and he may need oxygen. Pieces of spine, poisonous tissue and other foreign matter will have to be removed. An anti-tetanus injection is advisable and stitches may be necessary in a bad case. An antidote for Stonefish venom has been developed in Australia.

At Singapore the local fishermen used to bring me four or five Stone-fish from time to time as exhibits for the Aquarium. Then there came a call from America for a number of specimens to be used in research, so I offered one Malayan dollar apiece for them, hoping thereby to encourage the fishermen to make a special effort and maybe get me a couple of dozen during the next week. Came the dawn – and with it a party of fishermen carrying several cans containing approximately two hundred and fifty Stonefish. The competition had to be brought to an end at once, partly because of the cost but also because of the work involved in removing the venom glands to be dispatched in dry ice to America.

I was intrigued to know how they had managed to collect so many of these fish in so short a space of time, so as soon as time permitted I went out to the islands to investigate. It appeared that all the small boys had been mobilized and that they dived down, put a hand under a Stonefish and gripped it by its pelvic fins, returning to the surface waving it aloft – and remember, those fins by which the boys held them were armed with small spines containing the frightful venom. They did this for me several times and I photographed them. Not once did a boy come up empty handed. The mind boggles at the number of Stonefish there must be down there. One man on Pulau Sudong had a bad limp bequeathed to him by a Stonefish twenty years previously and he described his experience. I had been fishing around happily in those reefs but after that time any bit of stone had to be regarded with deep suspicion and prodded.

Stargazers are unusual in having venomous spines on their shoulders. This does not refer to astronomers but to the fishes of the family Uranoscopidae (Latinized Greek but still stargazers). Their eyes are set in such a position that they look forever upward, but not for stars. They sit around on the sea bed gazing up at whatever passes above them, hoping it will be food. The supracleithrum – the uppermost in the rather complex group of shoulder bones already mentioned – has a stout, sharp spine upon it, over which is a large, loosely fitting cone of tissue. The space between the bone and the cone is filled with venom and the whole thing is covered by the skin of the fish. Because of the shape of the fish these spines are at about its widest part, so anything trying to pick it up is likely to press on the spines, which break through the skin of both fish and aggressor while venom passes up the grooves on the lower sides of the spines, causing deep regret. As with the scorpion-fish, the sting proves fatal only occasionally, probably due as much to the condition of the victim as to the venom. In the event that the enemy does not press on these spines, the stargazer has a pair of electric organs behind the eyes to add discouragement. It is likely however that these are primarily used for knocking out food organisms that pass over it.

Wherever any of these venomous species are likely to occur, do not paddle or wade without footwear. Avoid holes and crevices. Do not lift up the feet and put them down again – even shoes may be pierced that way. Shuffle the feet along to push unpleasant things out of the way. A stick to prod ahead of you is a good idea.

There are some free-swimming fish that have poison of some sort

Most venomous of all fish is the Poison Stonefish, *Synanceja verrucosa*. Twelve spines along its back, showing white in this photo are provided with large bags of poison on each side. There are smaller spines below,

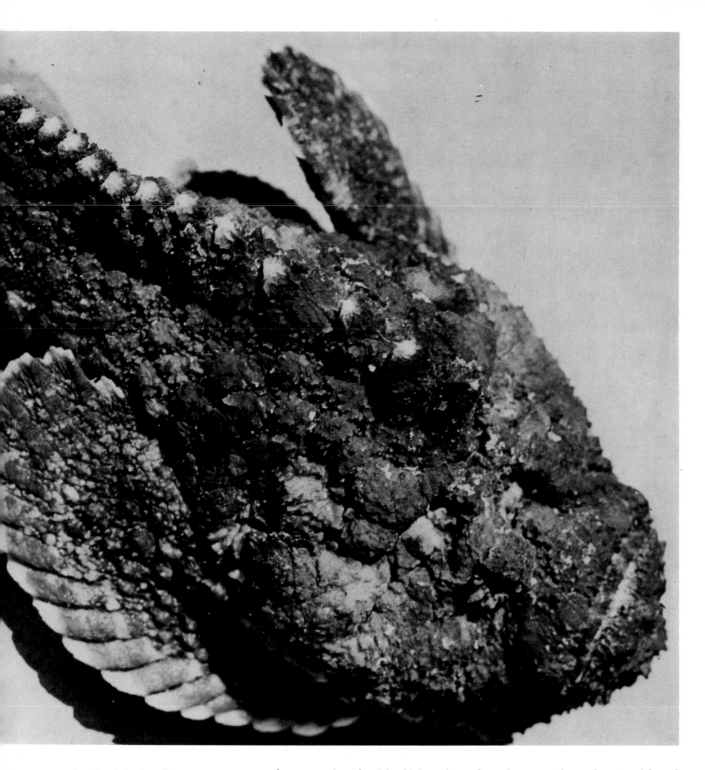

on anal and pelvic fins. Because of its rough skin and brown colour the fish is practically invisible among rocks. It may be trodden upon or handled by accident causing agony and possibly crippling the victim.

or another associated with their spines, but these need not be considered dangerous unless they are handled. For example surgeonfish (family Acanthuridae) have on each side of the tail a forward-pointing spine like a knife blade, that folds down into a slot when not in use. It is raised in self defence and it has been asserted that it can be used aggressively to kill other fish as food, though I must admit to being sceptical of this, having kept them with other species in aquaria. That it is mainly defensive is shown by the fact that it is often accompanied by a patch of colour as a warning signal. We cannot well expect more than that, so if we get wounded by a surgeonfish we have no one to blame but ourselves.

Electric fish

Brief mention was made in the previous chapter of the electric organs possessed by the stargazer. These are rather complicated structures occupying an oval area just behind each eye; indeed, the organ is a modified part of certain of the eye muscles. The electricity is discharged by means of a series of plates, each formed from a single muscle fibre, and can give a quite violent shock.

However, this is not by any means the only fish able to do this. Electrical impulses are produced in several quite unrelated groups and evolved in different ways, although all operating on a principle rather like that in the wet battery we use in cars. Sometimes the impulses are sent out as a kind of radar, bouncing back to the fish and keeping it informed of its surroundings; in others the energy is delivered as a knockout blow for prey or enemies. Most are to be found in fresh water, but in the sea there are some that make themselves felt.

Many of the rays make use of some kind of electricity, even the common Skate that we use as food, though I doubt if the fishermen who handle them regularly are aware of it. After being in a trawl along with some tons of other fish and tipped out on deck, the ray has already given whatever shocks it can and is exhausted. In any case the electric cells along each side of the tail of an ordinary ray are capable of producing only a feeble current.

The electric rays (family Torpedinidae), on the other hand, have highly developed organs at the base of each pectoral fin (that is, towards the centre of the disc) that occupy large kidney-shaped areas on the upper surface.

Parts of muscles, skin and nerves take part in these organs. Each consists of a large number – maybe three or four hundred – hexagonal cells, suggesting a honeycomb, filled with a clear, jelly-like substance. The walls of the cells are of fibrous tissue. Each is divided again into smaller compartments within each of which lies a plate which has a group of fine nerves attached to one side of it. This is the negative side; the other side is positive. The nerves from all the plates unite and eventually join the main nerve that supplies the whole organ. The elec-

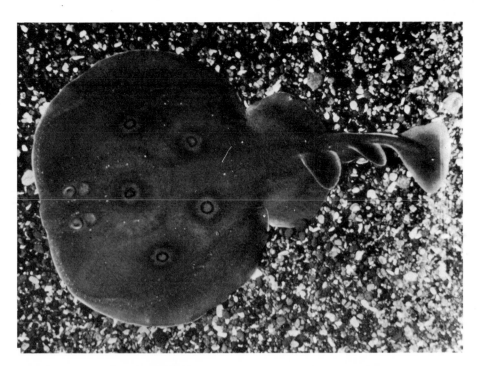

Right The Eyed Electric Ray, *Torpedo torpedo,* is common in the Mediterranean and was depicted in the mosaic pavement shown on page 45. The electric organs lie in the kidney-shaped areas that surround the outermost of the blue spots.

Below One of the largest of the electric rays, *Torpedo marmorata,* has a pattern that blends well with the sea floor on which it lies. It may be found in quite shallow water and gives an unpleasant sensation when stepped upon with bare feet. Its shock is not as violent as that of some smaller species.

tric current passes from the upper positive surface of the organ to the lower negative side. It has all the properties we normally expect, including the magnetizing of iron and the decomposing of other metals. It is transmitted through steel instruments such as knives and spears, through copper and bronze and of course through water.

There is no doubt that this property is used to stun other fish as food. The electric rays are sluggish creatures that lie half buried in sand or mud and are built, like other rays, for collecting their food from the bottom. What better than to knock out their quarry and then pick it up at leisure? That this is so has been shown by examining their stomach contents, which often include whole, intact fish without any marks of savaging upon them.

The first shock given by one of these rays is stronger than those that come after. In a large specimen it can amount to about a hundred volts which, in water, can stun a man. Subsequent shocks are progressively feebler, for the energy is soon exhausted. The fish must rest for a while, to recharge its batteries.

Electric rays are often found in quite shallow water and, being concealed, are likely to be trodden upon. Even a small one gives a most unpleasant sensation, while a large one can throw you down. Females often move into the shallows to give birth to their young (like the sting rays, they are viviparous). But some species can descend to a depth of 300 fathoms.

The largest species is the American *Torpedo occidentalis*, known there as the Crampfish, which may attain a weight of some 200 pounds. The best known is *T. marmoratus*, which is found in the Mediterranean and down the African coast to the Cape. In the Indian Ocean is found a closely related form, *T. sinus-persici*.

T. torpedo was known to the Romans who were ignorant of electricity except through this fish, through lightning and, in another form, through amber. Since it came into the category of magical things it was recommended as a remedy for various ailments. It is rather strikingly marked, with five large, black-edged, blue eye-spots on the back. Another large electric ray is *T. nobiliana*, which may be 4 feet across but gives a very feeble shock.

There are many more. Some of them are quite small, such as the Numbfish, genus *Narcine*, which has the spiracles close behind the eyes instead of at a distance as in *Torpedo*. These are common around American coasts. Another group of small rays is *Narke*, which has only one dorsal fin instead of the usual two. These are to be found in the Indo-Pacific from South Africa to Japan, but just to show that size is not everything, they can give a much nastier shock than some of the big ones.

Electric rays are, in texture, soft, flabby creatures that do not commend themselves to any but gourmets as delicacies, though some of them are indeed very good to eat. With all their galvanic powers they cannot be regarded as aggressive – just don't step on them. It is nice to record as a final word that, so far as I can discover, no human has ever been killed by one.

A Stargazer, *Uranoscopus scaber*, looks forever upward, with its mouth also upturned, for food that may come from above. It also watches for enemies which it can deter by means of a mild electric shock or a poison spine on each shoulder.

Sea serpents

From time immemorial there have been reports of a great sea serpent that rises enormously from the waves, swimming very improbably with vertical undulations, rearing aloft a long neck with a scarlet crest, supporting a head with immense eyes, horns and sometimes whiskers.

Over and over again something has been washed ashore that looked as if it might be the remains of such a creature, but always it has turned out to be something less impressive – most commonly the decomposing corpse of an unfortunate Basking Shark (inoffensive in life but somewhat offensive to the nostrils in a state of putrefaction).

We know very little about this sea serpent, for it has never been clearly photographed, never been drawn by anyone with combined zoological knowledge and artistic skill, never been measured and dissected by scientists. There are those who doubt whether any such thing really exists. But if it does, there is one thing we do know about it for certain – it is not a serpent.

There are sea serpents, but the traditional monster is not one of them. Real sea serpents are, as the name implies, snakes that live in the sea. About fifty species of these are known, all too small to give rise to any fables about monsters. An ordinary length is 4 or 5 feet, with many a good deal smaller and the largest growing on occasion to 8 feet. They all belong to the family Hydrophidae which is closely related to the well-known cobras; and like the cobras they are highly venomous.

But sea snakes are not aggressive and the few casualties associated with them are practically always due to accident or carelessness on the part of the human being concerned. They can be handled freely and will never deliberately bite unless subjected to rough treatment.

A few years ago I became quite well acquainted with a species of sea snake called *Laticauda laticaudatus*, which is of great interest because it forms a sort of stepping-stone from the cobras to other sea snakes. Like the cobras it lays eggs and of course comes out of the sea to do this. But the tail is flattened from side to side to help propel it through the water and the broad scales along the lower side of the body which a land snake uses in crawling across the ground are much reduced.

Not far from Singapore is a small island with elaborately eroded rocks which are particularly favoured by *Laticauda*. One or more is usually to be found in every sizeable cranny and others are swimming in the shallow coral-strewn waters around. Once out of the water they could be picked up with ease, since they cannot move so fast as other snakes over land. Consequently it was possible to get good still photographs and cine films by placing them where they were required. They were most obliging and never made any hostile movement.

One odd thing I discovered was that a female coiled over her eggs in a crevice would make quite a loud squeak if she was touched with the end of a twig. The squeak was accompanied by a sharp movement but I was not able to discern whether the sound was produced by the scales against the sides of the crevice, in the manner of a slate pencil, or by air expelled by the lung. When one day I took a party of students with a professor from the University out to the island I demonstrated this phenomenon, but to my surprise nobody believed it—the professor insisted that I was producing the sound by ventriloquism. Thus are Galileo and I pilloried with scepticism and approbrium.

All the rest of the sea snakes are entirely aquatic, never coming out of the sea. The lung reaches almost the whole length of the animal and holds enough air to enable the snake to swim under water for several hours before coming to the surface for replenishment. The nostrils are provided with valves that seal them shut while below the surface. Mostly the body as well as the tail is flattened from side to side but there is considerable variation. *Microcephalophis gracilis* has a quite thick and sturdy body that forms a steady base upon which a long thin neck

Olao Magno Gotho, Archbishop of Uppsala, visualized the sea serpent like this.

This great Oar Fish may be the
kind of creature behind the myth
of the sea serpent.

with a tiny head can poise itself and strike at its prey like a cobra. This one is said to feed entirely on eels, but I found that as often as not the prey was a 'pearl fish' (*Carapus*) which is elongate but is not strictly speaking an eel. *Carapus* spends a good deal of time inside another animal, the sea cucumber or trepang, and it is literally sticking its neck out when the sea snake strikes.

Another account credits this species with feeding on fish eggs which it digs from deep down in the coral sand. I do not know of a fish that buries its eggs in the sand, so I cannot comment on this.

As all these true sea snakes have completely lost the broad scales of the underside used for locomotion by land snakes, and the tail is usually curved downwards like a stern oar, they are quite unable to progress on dry ground. They are viviparous, the young being born under water and able to swim as soon as discharged.

Many of the species are to be found swimming well out to sea. One kind has sometimes been seen in large shoals (probably congregating for breeding) in the middle of the Indian Ocean. During the time when I was curator of the public aquarium at Singapore the Soviet research ship *Vitjaz* made a call and among the interesting things Dr Parin and his team had collected was a pair of these ocean-going sea snakes, *Pelamys platurus*, which were presented to the aquarium. They were very beautiful creatures, striped longitudinally with deep, rich brown on the back, red shading into yellow on the sides and a group of black spots on the broadly flattened tail. The head of *Pelamys* is larger than in most sea snakes and the gape of the mouth is considerable. Clearly it is able to eat comparatively large animals, but although our pair stayed with us longer than one would expect under the circumstances we were not able to persuade them to take any food.

Snakes of any kind are notoriously difficult to induce to feed when brought into captivity, and the marine species generally run true to form. At Singapore we tried many times to keep specimens of *Hydrophis* – the best-known genus – without success, until one day we put a small specimen, scarcely a foot long, into a tank with some small fish. We did not expect it to attack the fish and indeed it did not, but when we fed them on the usual diet of chopped squid, fish and ox heart the little snake joined in. From then on it fed regularly, mainly on chopped fish, and grew into a fine specimen; when I left Singapore four years later it was well over 4 feet long and very tame.

A typical sea snake, *Hydrophis fasciatus,* is helpless out of water as it lacks the special scales needed for progression on land and it has a tail specially flattened for swimming.

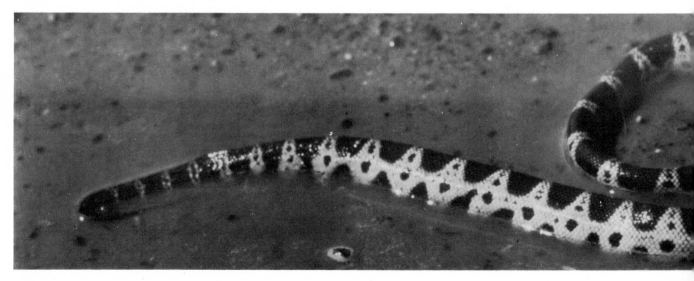

Most sea snakes have a rather small head in proportion to the body and the mouth is so small that many of them would find it difficult to bite a large creature like ourselves, unless perhaps on the little finger or toe. When swimmers have been bitten they have usually been standing around in areas where a strong tide-race or a wind-driven swell threatens to sweep the snake ashore. In such a situation the snake may try to anchor itself by hanging on to the nearest object and if that happens to be a human foot the owner thereof will need hospital treatment.

During the monsoon the Straits of Malacca often provide the conditions for such incidents and the research centre at Penang some years ago developed an anti-venom effective against sea snake bites, which is made available to hospitals in the area. No time must be lost in getting treatment, for this bite is virulent. Old ideas about cutting the wound to make it bleed and sucking out the venom are not effective – they waste time and may increase the danger. If it is practicable a tourniquet between the wound and the heart is the only immediate aid that should be given and the patient should be encouraged to keep quite still while being rushed to hospital. The ligature should be released a little occasionally as it is only intended to slow the blood in the veins and not to stop the circulation.

Perhaps the most dangerous thing about sea snake bites is that they are often not felt, or the prick is so slight that it is soon forgotten, for no great pain is produced. But a little while later there comes weakness in the legs, lockjaw much as in tetanus, and shortage of breath. The patient may go into a coma and live for some time before the effect on the lungs brings death.

Swimmers in the United States and Europe have no need to worry about sea snakes because they are not found in the Atlantic and Mediterranean nor in the North Pacific. Their main centre is around the East Indies and Philippines where most of the species occur; from there they are distributed along the coasts to the west as far as East Africa and to the east as far as southern Japan, becoming fewer in species as they go. The oceanic species *Pelamys platurus* already mentioned has crossed the Pacific and is plentiful from El Salvador south to Peru.

Compared with other creatures inhabiting the same waters and with the chances of being bitten by a terrestrial snake in the same regions, the sea serpents can be put far down on our list of tropical hazards.

The head of a sea snake, showing the valves which close the nostrils when the animal is under water. Air is taken into a lung extending almost the whole length of the body.

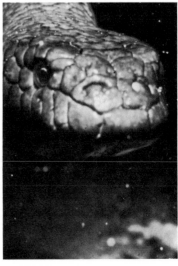

Further Reading

The Life of Sharks by Paul Budker. Weidenfeld and Nicolson, London, 1971.

Shark Attack by R. J. Coppleson. Angus and Robertson, Sydney, 1962.

About Sharks and Shark Attack by D. H. Davies. Shuter and Shuter, Pietermaritzburg, 1964.

Stingfish and Seafarer by H. M. Evans. Faber and Faber, London, 1943.

Sharks and Survival by P. W. Gilbert. D. C. Heath, Boston, 1963.

Dangerous Marine Animals by B. W. Halstead. Cornell Maritime Press, 1959.

Poisonous and Venomous Marine Animals of the World by B. W. Halstead. US Govt. Printing Office, Washington, 1965.

The Invertebrates by L. H. Hyman. McGraw Hill, New York, 1940.

The Natural History of Sharks by Lineaweaver and Backus. Andre Deutsch, London, 1970.

Harpoon at a Venture by Gavin Maxwell. Rupert Hart-Davis, London, 1952.

Shadows in the Sea by McCormick, Allen and Young. Sidgwick and Jackson, London, 1963.

Acknowledgements

Photographs are reproduced by courtesy of the following:
Trustees of the British Museum (Natural History) 13 (top), 13 (bottom), 14, 15; Marineland of Florida 67, 68, 74–75, 94–95, 103, 106; National Maritime Museums 120–121.
Sources of Photographs:
COLOUR
Ardea Photographics – P. Morris 108–109, Ron Taylor front jacket, 17 (bottom), 62, 63, 84–85, 88 (top), back jacket (top), John Wightman 88–89; Jacana – R. Fenaux 21, A. Visage 93; Frank W. Lane 51 (bottom), Frank W. Lane – W. T. Miller 17 (top), Laurence E. Perkins 51 (top); Photo Aquatics – Hansen 97, back jacket (bottom), P. Kopp 88 (bottom), 96; Popperfoto 24 (top), 92; Seaphot – Walter Deas 24–25, 50–51, 58–59, John Lythgoe 100–101, Peter Scoones 20 (bottom), 104–105; Z.E.F.A. – Grossauer 32, Paul Kamper 24 (bottom), Rosmarie Pierer 20 (top), back jacket (centre), A. Thau 54–55.
BLACK AND WHITE
Heather Angel 22–23, 39 (bottom), 40 (top), 40 (bottom), 43, 113; Ardea Photographics – Ron Taylor 78, 125, Valerie Taylor 42; Bruce Coleman Ltd. – Des and Jen Bartlett 86–87, Bruce Coleman 124–125, Russ Kinne title page, 34–35, Allan Power 39 (top), 56–57 (top); A. Fraser-Brunner 76 (top), 76–77; Hamlyn Group Picture Library 45, 120–121; Frank W. Lane 46, Frank W. Lane – J. Howes 111, Marineland of Florida 67, 68, 74–75, 94–95, 103, 106, Erling Sivertsen 48 (left), R. F. LeSueur 48 (right), Fred H. Wylie 53; Popperfoto 61, 65, 73, 122–123; Seaphot 98, Dick Clarke 107, Jean Deas 102–103, Walter Deas 52, 56–57 (bottom), 76 (bottom), 81, Colin Doeg 64, Werner Frei 116–117, J. David George 13 (top), 13 (bottom), 14, 15, Geoff Harwood 26–27, Peter Saw 114–115, Peter Scoones 110, Stevenino 118–119; John Topham Ltd. 36; Douglas P. Wilson 10–11, 16, 19, 28–29, 112, 117; Z.E.F.A. – D. Baglin 37.
The choice and arrangement of the illustrations in this book were made by the publisher.

Index

Page numbers in italic refer to illustrations

Acanthaster planci 53, *55*
Acanthocybium 94, *95–97*
Aeolids 38, *40*, *41*
Aglaeophenia 21, 26
Algae 12, 43, 100
Amphiprion 32
Architeuthis 47–51
Asthenosoma varium 56
Aurelia 23, 35

Bacteria 12
Barracudas 95–97
Basking Shark 64, 120
Batrachoides didactylus 110
Bêche-de-mer 52, 57
Black Long-spined Urchin 54
Black-tipped Shark 60, 76
Blanket Octopus 31, 47
Blue Shark 78–79
Bluebottle *24*, 30
Blue-ringed Octopus 47, *50*
Blue-spotted Stingray *101*
Bonito 95
Bonnet Shark 79
Boxfish 102
Broadbill Swordfish 82, 99

Carapus 57, 124
Carcharhinid sharks *65*, 66–70, *74*
Carcharhinidae 66
Carcharhinus gangeticus 77
  leucas 66, 77
  longimanus 78
  menisorrah 77
  sorrah 60
Carcharias arenarius 86, *88*
  taurus 68, 83
  tricuspidatus 83
Carcharodon carcharias 63, 82–83
Carpet sharks 74, *80*
Carukia barnesi 22, 34
Carukiosis 34
Catfish 106
Centrostephanus 56
Cetorhinus maximus 64
Charybdea rastoni 35
Chironex fleckeri 22, 34
Chiropsalmus quadrigatus 34
Ciguatera 100–102
Ciguatoxin 102
Cnidaria 26, 31
Cnidoblasts 19, 26
Coelenterates 26
Compass Jelly *21*
Cone shells 41–42
Conus gloriamaris 41
  textile 42
Coral 36, *37*
Coryzichthys 110
Cotton spinners 57
Crabs 43
Crampfish 119

Crocodiles 86–90
Crocodylus porosus 86
Crown-of-thorns *52*, 53, *55*
Cub sharks *see* Carcharhinid sharks
Cube jellies 33–35
Cubomedusae 33, 34
Cuttlefish 44
Cyanea 18, *22*, 23, 31

Dactylometra quinquecirrah 31
Dasyatis pastinaca 104, *113*
Diadema antillarum 54
  savignyi 54
  setosum 54
Diatoms 9
Dinoflagellates 9–12, *16*
Disc jellies 31, 33
Dogfish 62, 66
Dolphins 90
Dragonfish 111

Echinodermata 52
Echinothrix 56
Echinus esculenta 54
Electric organs 114, 116–117
Electric rays 116–119
Elkhorn Coral 26
Estuarine Crocodile *71*, 86
Eyed Electric Ray *117*

Fibulia nolitangere 15
Fire coral 26, *27*

Galapagos Shark 73, 74
Galeocerdo cuvier 74
Ganges Shark 77
Gharial 90
Giant Bass 91, *92*, 94
Giant Clam *39*, 42–43
Giant Squid 47–51
Ginglymostoma cirrhatum 74
  ferrugineum 74
Glory-of-the-Sea Cone 41
Gonionemus vertens 26, 30
Gonyaulax 11–12
Great Barracuda 97
Great Hammerhead Shark 79
Great White Shark *63*, *71*, 82–83, 104
Greater Weever 110
Grey Reef Shark 77
Groupers 91
Guitarfish 103
Gymnodinium 11
Gymnothorax 95

Hammerhead sharks 79–80
Harpoon 41
Holothuria scabra 57
Horse mackerel 68
Hydroids *17*, *21*, 30
Hydrophidae 120
Hydrozoa 26
Hydrophis fasciatus 124
Hydrozoa 26

Ink sac 47
Irukandji 33–34
Istiophorus americanus 99
  gladius 99
Isurus glaucus 82
  oxyrinchus 80

Jellyfish 18–35

Killer Whale *71*, *87*, *89*, 90
Kraken 47

Lamna nasus 80
Lamnid sharks 80
Lampreys 102
Laticauda laticaudatus 120–121
Lesser Weever 107, 110
Lionfish *105*, 111
Lobsters 43
Luminescence 12, *16*, 35, 64
Lytocarpus 17

Mackerel Shark 80
Mackerel sharks 63
Mako 82, 83
Marlins 99
Mauve Jelly 35
Medusae 23–24, 31
Microcephalophis gracilis 121–124
Microciona prolifera 15
Millepora alcicornis 26
  dichotoma 21
  platyphylla 26
Molluscs 38–43, 44
Moray eels 91–95
Muraena helena 95
Muraenesox cinereus 95
Mussel *39*

Narcine 119
Narke 119
Needle-spined urchin 54
Nematocysts 18–23, 30, 33, 41, 47
Noctiluca 11, 12, *16*
Nomeus 31
Nudibranch molluscs 23
Numbfish 119
Nurse Shark *73*, 74

Oar Fish *122–123*
Octopus maculosus 47, *50*
Octopuses 44–47, 49, *51*
Orcinus orca 90
Orectolobid sharks 74

Paracentrotus lividus 54
Paralytic shellfish poisoning 10
'Pearl fish' 124
Pedicellaria 56, 57
Pelagia noctiluca 35
Pelamys platurus 124, 125
Pennaria 26
Physalia physalis 24, 30–31, 47
  utriculus *24*, 30
Plankton 9, 26
Plotosus 106
Polyps 26, 31, *36*, 41
Porbeagle 80, 83
Portuguese Man-of-War 24, *25*, 30–31, 34, 47
Prionace glauca 78
Pristis 103
Promicrops lanceolatus 91, *92*
Protozoa 8–12, *16*
Pterois 111, *112*
  antennata *105*
  volitans 111, *112*
Pufferfish 100

Pyrodinium 11

Rays 102–103, 116, 119
Rhincodon typus 64
Rhinobatos 103

Sagartia elegans 16, *28–29*, 36
Sailfish 99
Sand sharks *68*, 83, *88*
Sawfish 103, *106*
Scorpionfish 102, *108–109*, 110
Scyliorhinus stellaris 62
Sea anemones 16, *17*, 26, *28–29*, *32*, 36
Sea cucumbers 52, 53, 57
Sea hares 38
Sea Needle 54
Sea Nettle 31
Sea serpents 120, *121*
Sea slugs 38, *40*
Sea snakes 120–125
Sea stars 52–54
Sea urchins 52, 54–57, *58–59*
Serranus 91
Sharks 60–86, 102
Siphonophores 30
Skate 116
Spearfish 99
Sperm Whale 48, 49
Sphyraena 95–97

sphyraena 97
Sphyrna blochi 79
  lewini 80
  mokarran 79, 80
  tiburo 79
  zygaena 80
Spicules *13*, 14, *15*
Sponge fisher's disease 16, 36
Sponges 12–16, *17*, 36
Spotted Dogfish 62, 80
Spur Dog 60
Squalus acanthias 62
Squids 44, 47–51
Starfish *see* Sea stars
Stargazers 114, 116, *118*
Stingrays 102–104, *107*, *113*
Stinging cells *see* Nematocysts
Stonefish 102, 111–114, *115*
Surgeonfish 115
Swordfish 82, 97–99
Synanceja horrida 111
  verrucosa 115

Taeniura lymma 101
Tamoya haplonema 35
Tedania 15, *17*
Tetrodotoxin 100
Thalassophryne 110
Tiger Shark 74–77

Toadfish 110
Torpedinidae 116
Torpedo marmorata 117, 119
  nobiliana 119
  occidentalis 119
  sinus-persici 119
  torpedo 117, 119
Toxopneustes pileolus 56–57
Trachinus draco 110
  vipera 110
Trepang 57
Tridacna 39, 42–43
Tripneustes ventricosus 54
Trunkfish 102
Tuna 68, 95
Turkeyfish 111

Uranoscopidae 114
Uranoscopus scaber 119

Wahoo *94*, 97
Weevers 102, 106–110
Whale Shark 64
Whaler 78–79, 83
White Shark *see* Great White Shark
White-tipped Shark *76*, 78, *88*
Wobbegong 74, *80*

Xiphias gladius 82, 99